The Haunted Universe

Other D. Scott Rogo titles published by Anomalist Books

A Casebook of Otherworldly Music
A Psychic Study of the Music of the Spheres
In Search of the Unknown
Miracles
On the Track of the Poltergeist
Our Psychic Potentials
The Search for Yesterday

THE HAUNTED UNIVERSE

BY D. SCOTT ROGO

ANOMALIST BOOKS
San Antonio • New York

The Haunted Universe
Copyright © 1977 by D. Scott Rogo

Anomalist Books edition: 2006
ISBN: 1933665157

Originally published by Signet/New American Library in 1977.
Reprinted with permission of the Rogo Family Trust.

Cover image: Kristian Birchall
Cover design by Ansen Seale

All rights reserved, including the right to reproduce this book or portions thereof in any form whatsoever. For information, go to anomalistbooks.com or write to:

Anomalist Books
5150 Broadway #108
San Antonio, TX 78209

Anomalist Books
PO Box 577
Jefferson Valley, NY 10535

To Martin Ebon,
in thanks for his help and support

ACKNOWLEDGMENTS

Writing this book has been no easy matter. It has been an especially hard chore because of the bizarre material covered. So I am especially indebted to several people who advised me during the writing. First to Dr. Berthold Schwarz who supplied me with a gold mine of back issues of the *Flying Saucer Review* and kindly gave me copies of all his UFO writings. Both Raymond Bayless and Vincent Gaddis lent me files full of case reports on Fortean happenings, and I am indebted to the writings of John Keel and Ivan Sanderson whose work and views I have so often quoted in the book.

Finally, I would like to thank those few "respectable" parapsychologists and colleagues who urged me *not* to write this book, fearing it would adversely reflect on both me and the field. It was their timidity and reticence that helped me realize how important getting this material out in the open really is!

CONTENTS

Chapter

1	The Cosmic Interface	1
2	The Mystery of Teleportation	7
3	Mysteries and Miracles	33
4	UFOs: Space Vehicles or Psychic Entities?	80
5	Pascagoula Revisited: The Psychic Story	122
6	The Cosmic Invaders	135
7	A Psychic Look at Forteana	147
	Bibliography	164

CHAPTER 1

The Cosmic Interface

By inclination I am a pretty reserved fellow. Having spent my last several years studying ESP, psychokinesis, and other psychic phenomena both in and out of parapsychology laboratories, I've learned many invaluable lessons. I've learned how people often distort, elaborate, or even lie about their personal experiences. I've learned that theories shouldn't be propagated unless there is a way of testing them. And it is Western orthodox science that points the way to how proper research should be done. I've also learned that the "wilder" the claim someone makes about an ability or experience the more likely it is that the claim is false. But despite all this, I've been so intrigued by the many times I have encountered the unknown that I doubt if my pursuit of it will ever end.

Like many professionals in the field, I'm sometimes entangled in a psychic jungle. I carry out neat and trim ESP experiments or conduct a rigid, skeptical investigation of a haunting or poltergeist. I examine witnesses, record testimony, take measurements, and so forth *ad infinitum*. In fact, while I was once carrying out one of these respectable experiments, a psychiatrist friend looked at me and said, "You know, I've found that parapsychologists are just like everybody else—rather dull."

He's right!

Sometimes in our fight to be respectable we do become dull. Enmeshed in statistics, experimental designs, control groups and variables, psychic phenomena often lose much of their wonderland—excuse the term—aura. We fail to see the natural implications of what we are studying. If ESP and mind-over-matter do exist, what lies beyond, out there in our barely understood universe or within the recesses of our own minds? Back in Victorian England psychic investigations were labeled as attempts to "naturalize the supernatural," and it was at that time that psychic research became a rather drab affair. To date, parapsychologists have only been concerned with the study of two groups of phenomena: extrasensory perception and psychokinesis.

This is a very limited outlook, for there are mysteries far beyond the "psychic" which we have not even begun to examine: the perpetually elusive UFO and the wild *psychic* manifestations recorded during their activity; supernatural but well-evidenced aerial lights and apparitions which have appeared during religious revivals; new dimensions of space contacted by those experiencing out-of-the-body travel; and "weeping" pictures and statues which have been recorded for centuries and which have baffled scientists and theologians alike. Whole new universes open up through the dimensions of psychic and preternatural phenomena.

Are these phenomena paranormal or delusional? I think these weird manifestations are very real and have an intimate bearing on the nature of ESP and PK in general.

Then why hasn't the public been told of them? Well, for one thing, there has been no organized attempt to study these phenomena scientifically. Unlike ESP and psychokinesis, which can be studied in the laboratory, the evidence for the existence of UFOs, miracles, weeping pictures, and teleportation still rests only on disjointed observations. A few writers—such as Ivan Sanderson, and before him Charles Fort, as well as the always intriguing John Keel—have written about *some* of these mysteries. But, as anyone can tell you, journalists and writers aren't very convincing. They don't have what in communication studies is called "ethos," which can roughly be translated as "inherent credibility." Writers just don't cause much commotion. If a journalist writes that a chemical in the brain might cause chronic depression, no one pays much attention. But if the same thing is mentioned by a PhD in psychology, who probably does not have any great knowledge of neurophysiology, headlines scream, every scientist in the country as well as his lab assistant is asked to comment, and the tabloid press rushes in for the story.

Another reason for the lack of interest in these subjects can be laid to a conspiracy of silence and ignorance. Few scientists, even parapsychologists, are aware of the above-mentioned phenomena, and fewer yet are versed in their study. A few years ago if you mentioned ESP to a group of psychologists you would have gotten icy stares and perhaps a few obscene under-the-breath comments. This has all changed now that parapsychology has become respectable. But just mention the Fatima miracles, or UFOs, or weeping madonnas, or mysterious lights in the sky to parapsychologists and they will out-icy-stare any group of academicians!

In this book I am going to break through the inhibitions we work under in parapsychology. I'm not going to be reserved or worry about respectability in what I'm going to say or report. For years I have been interested in much more than just ESP and PK. I've seen a lot of that over the years. I've watched psychics work their wonders in the lab; after a six-year search I've had the good fortune to observe a rampaging poltergeist; I've seen animals react to unseen out-of-body visitors. But this is only the beginning of what lies out there in the strange Universe; mysteries are just waiting to be tracked down. And I'm going to report some of those mysteries now!

As I hinted above, I've encountered psychic phenomena several times during the course of my work. I've lived in a haunted house where the bed would shake under me; I've stalked poltergeists galore; and I've seen a red light dancing about my room when an astral traveler was attempting to visit me. All of these experiences got me to wondering. We certainly seem capable of creating some strange things in the world. Take the poltergeist, for instance. A family will suddenly find itself in the midst of a nightmare as objects fly about, windows are smashed to bits, and household items disappear and reappear mysteriously. Yet we know that these rages are usually caused by the mind of a frustrated youngster venting his violence unconsciously through mind-over-matter. The mind, it seems, has the actual ability to move things and—even more spectacularly—dematerialize and rematerialize them as well. So, my thoughts continued, what else are we creating in this strange world of ours? Are our unconscious minds creating all sorts of disturbances around us without our even knowing it?

A very good example of this occurred right in my home not too long ago. I had just spent the day working on a chapter about how we use psychokinesis (mind-over-matter) unconsciously. I finished my work by 10:00 P.M. and went to bed. My house is a nice, old-fashioned tract home. There is nothing peculiar about it—there are no ghosts lurking about. It's just a dull old house. Yet, that night at about 3:00 A.M. a tenant of mine decided to drop in for a chat after work. Using his house key, he wandered in and, a few seconds later, had the fright of his life! As he meandered through the house, a chair suddenly lunged from behind him by itself, pulling away from a table noisily. Isn't it odd that as I slept, my tenant was greeted by the very type of PK effect I'd been writing about all day?

If the mind can do this much, it can do much more. Within the power of the mind and body may lie the key with which we might solve all sorts of mysteries that continually haunt our world. We see UFOs in the sky, but no one ever seems able to shoot one down. We have long hunted for Bigfoot and a host of kindred abominable snowmen, but they always seem to vanish, gremlinlike, while we are hot on their trail. Today, apparitions of the Virgin Mary appear to Catholics and Protestants alike, just as we have been led to believe they appeared in biblical days. Is our planet haunted by intelligent beings beyond our own intelligence? Or are we playing a grand psychic charade? Are we haunting our own universe through the psychic abilities of our minds?

A very good example of just this sort of phenomenon occurred during the First World War. On September 29, 1914, the *London Evening News* ran a story by one of Great Britain's best short-story writers, Arthur Machen, entitled, "The Angel of Mons." With his usual flair for fantasy, Machen told a tale about how at the Battle of Mons, which the English had recently fought in France, St. George and his phantom bowmen angelically protected the English troops. Although Machen staunchly insisted that the story was totally fictional, it wasn't long before phantom bowmen were actually being reported from all parts of Europe.

I don't believe that the soldiers who saw the phantom bowmen were hallucinating. I think they actually *created* these phantoms. Their wishes and fantasies about Machen's wonderful tale actually took on a physical reality. The bowmen really were there, protecting them. They were not angelic hosts, but psychic creations of their own minds.

The possibility and evidence that we are actually populating our universe with psychic creations and beings will serve as the topic for this book. I have no doubt that such things as UFOs and "monsters" are physical realities ... realities totally apart from our minds. But I believe that they are psychic realities as well. These enigmatic creatures and vehicles are haunting our planet, *but through the power of our minds* we are imitating them and creating more and more of them. For every UFO that flits through the sky, many more are created by the psyche. The same principle holds true for many other puzzles of nature. With this principle in mind, we can begin our psychic journey ... a journey along a cosmic interface.

Before beginning this meta-journey I would like to answer two questions the reader is sure to ask. This will help clarify my own position about the subjects I'm going to cover.

Question one: Do I believe all of the extraordinary events I'm reporting? The answer, basically, is yes. Often the testimony comes from a good source or from good witnesses. I've seen evidence of poltergeists, ESP, and hauntings, and I know that if *this* much is out there in our world or in our minds, even more bizarre things are distinctly possible. Some reports are not as well verified, but since they are on record they will be passed on to you. However, I will carefully point out any disparities in the evidence.

Question two: Do I really believe that the speculations I will be promoting are likely to turn out to be true? This is a trickier question. The book should be read like one of Marshall McLuhan's. As you know, McLuhan works from the premise that he is offering suggestions, possibilities, or just different ways of looking at things, and not necessarily his personal opinions. That is what I plan to do. I often have theories, which may be right or wrong, but I have no way of knowing the outcome. However, I would like to express them so that others can consider them as well.

But one thing is certain—this book is not being written for entertainment nor to make a fast buck by polluting the already overstocked book market on pop parapsychology and do-it-yourself miracles. I'm writing it with the firm conviction that many things exist around us that we are only beginning to become aware of and which conventional science and even conventional parapsychology are ignoring or overlooking. Nor am I throwing caution to the winds. I don't believe in psychic surgery, or that Kirlian photography reveals the aura, or in numerology or Santa Claus. What I *am* trying to present is a critical evaluation of a large body of anomalous experiences that go far beyond the world of the psychic into a world of observations about new universes, psychic UFOs, religious miracles, and the like. And I will do this cautiously, trying to evaluate the reports scientifically and openly, but never credulously.

As I said earlier, Ivan Sanderson was the first to devote a full-time career to the study of these encounters. He had a marvelous sense of humor, and in his book *Uninvited Visitors* he compared our potential search for knowledge to the various stages of insect growth. Let me borrow the analogy. Should we spend our time crawling caterpillar-like toward what may be a blind alley? Should we not instead confront problems that are more easily understood? Or not be bothered by scientific problems at all? Sanderson, who conceptualized our genetically enforced search for ultimate truth as the blind travels of a caterpillar, had a wonderful response to the argument that we had no free will in the matter:

> What's so bad about being a caterpillar anyway? Let us not forget that a caterpillar finally turns into the beautiful and free moth, who may have the ultimate satisfaction of giving birth! Personally, however, I prefer the life of a caterpillar. At least it eats and grows, and it does things. The moth does nothing but breed, get wet, and then die. What an egg does I could not care less! In fact, *me* for the larval stage—at least we are the ones who *do things*.

For a long time I've been crawling out of the parapsychology feeding ground to find richer leaves. And in the following pages you can crunch along with me.

CHAPTER 2

The Mystery of Teleportation

The concept that there are many universes intertwining with our own is an old one which, like the mythical phoenix, is periodically resurrected. But, as I indicated earlier, one shouldn't promote a theory unless there is a way of testing it. Sometimes this is impossible, but the least we can do is search around for evidence that is consistent with the theory.

If there are many worlds kaleidoscopically intermingling with our own, we can prove it only through our ability to contact them. Apparently some people have, but most never return to tell the story. These human tragedies are called "mysterious disappearances" and serve as the first rung on a tall ladder of evidence indicating that our world is only one of many which compose our universe. Take, for example, the Mount Glastonbury occurrences of the 1940s, in which there was a whole sequence of mysterious disappearances over a period of a few years. These reports have recently been disinterred by popular writer Brad Steiger.

The epidemic began on November 12, 1945, when Middie Rivers, a 75-year-old hunting guide, was leading a group of mountaineers through very familiar terrain. He was pacing just in front of the group when he suddenly disappeared without a trace. He was never found, despite the fact that the police as well as hundreds of volunteers hunted for him.

A year later, teen-aged Paula Weldon was the next victim to disappear in the same area in which Rivers vanished. She had gone on a hike to get away from her academic responsibilities at a local college; she was seen by several people at different points in her walk . . . until she simply vanished. Again volunteers massed for the search, police tracked down leads, rumors flew like deranged sparrows, but no Miss Weldon.

Exactly three years after the Weldon disappearance, James Tetford decided to visit Bennington, Vermont, which is situated very near Mount Glastonbury. Although he was seen to get on the proper bus by several witnesses, he never got off. As Steiger notes:

> A thorough investigation could reveal absolutely no clues to Tetford's strange disappearance. Several people saw him board the bus, but no one saw him get off the vehicle. It would seem impossible to vacate a bus enroute to its next station, either voluntarily or involuntarily, without being seen by the other passengers and the bus driver.

Steiger has traced two more disappearances which occurred in 1950 in the Bennington area. Eight-year-old Paul Jepson was left on the seat of his father's truck while he went on an errand. But when he returned ... Again there was a repeat of the Weldon investigation complete with volunteers, bloodhounds, police, and private investigators. I don't think I need recount the outcome of the search. In fact, it was reported that the dogs lost the track of the boy in the same area in which Paula Weldon had disappeared. Two weeks later, a teen-ager walked a half mile down a road to visit a friend in Bennington. She never arrived.

Now it is true that people disappear all the time. Crabby wives or nefarious creditors are often the cause. Many writers such as Steiger take great delight in cataloguing these cases and have speculated on some bizarre explanations for these disappearances. Everything from UFO abduction to holes in space have been blamed. This leads us back to what we said earlier—let us not promote theories without first figuring out a way to substantiate them. Let's not get science-fictiony or paranoid. The facts are simply that people do disappear and never show up again. Secondly, some of the disappearances seem to have no normal explanation. Why?

First, some occur under conditions that make abduction or desertion hardly likely. For example, a happily married and financially secure person sets out to walk to a liquor store a block away on a well-traveled street and is never seen again. On other occasions, as in the Mount Glastonbury epidemic, there are multiple disappearances. As Steiger congently comments:

The Mystery of Teleportation

No motive for murder could be determined in any of the seven cases. No ransom demands were ever received by any of the victims' family. No clues were ever found to explain the total disappearances of the victims . . . Each of the victims disappeared in the same season of the year in the same area of Mount Glastonbury.

Thank you, Mr. Steiger.

Needless to say, the casual reader may not be too impressed by these incidents of mysterious disappearance. I might add that until 1970 neither was I. Like so many others, it was easy for me to sit back complacently, assuring myself that eventually a normal explanation would be found for these inexplicable occurrences. (Scientists once thought the same about ESP, but they were wrong!)

It is one thing though to read and write about these disappearances, romanticizing or sensationalizing them at the same time. But it is an altogether different matter when one actually is face to face with one of these cases and becomes enmeshed in trying to untangle it. Since by profession I investigate strange things, usually psychic phenomena, it was only natural that eventually I would confront a mystery so bizarre and complex that it would go far beyond anything covered by my parapsychological training. It was a single strange disappearance that made me think twice about the phenomenon, and I have been thinking about it ever since.

The occurrence which has never before been published, concerned a woman named Danya, a rather pathetic young girl whose basic pastimes were shacking up with men, partying, and occasionally shooting up with drugs. I got to know Danya in 1970 when she was befriended by an acquaintance of mine named Mark; they spent several weeks together in a little house situated behind some trees on a fairly large lot on the outskirts of Los Angeles. The lot, which was flanked on one side by a bowling alley, on the other by a manufacturing plant, faced a major street, well traveled by automobiles, bicycles, and pedestrians.

One night in August, 1970, Danya went out to a party, leaving a group of friends behind at Mark's house. She returned at 12:15 A.M. People in the house heard a car door slam out in the street, and looking out from behind the curtains, saw Danya's dim outline walking toward them. They sat back to wait for her arrival, but she never arrived. She simply vanished at some point during the 150-foot walk from the street to the house.

Normal explanations for her disappearance do not hold water. Although her outline was dim, she was clearly recognized by those in the house. When we contacted the people who drove her home, they testified that they had dropped her off in front of the house and watched as she walked toward it before driving off. All the testimony adds up tight as a knot. Nor does rape or abduction seem a likely explanation. The street was well lighted, no struggle or screams were heard, and Danya was walking away from a major thoroughfare. Although Danya's past history would not lead one to believe that she was very reliable, I don't think she would have run away. She left her belongings at the house and deserted her best friend and traveling companion, who was also staying at the house.

Eventually the police were called in, but their investigation turned up nothing new. Everything points to a case of mysterious disappearance. According to the witnesses, Danya simply disappeared as she walked down a 150-foot path in a town where she knew almost no one. So ends the strange case of Danya.

Putting aside outlandish theories such as UFO abduction or antimatter machines, what happened to Paula Weldon, Paul Jepson, Danya, and many others? Obviously they went *somewhere*. But since they were never seen again, we can at least tentatively conclude that, *if in fact their disappearances were unnatural*, they somehow entered or were transported into a new universe.

I never put much stock in this theory until I was confronted by and investigated the case of Danya. But let us examine this theory. If people are popping into new dimensions, then we would expect that not only people but objects as well would pop in and out. And this is exactly what we do find.

There is a very rare form of psychic occurrence which has been labeled "instantaneous disappearance." In these cases, objects seem to vanish instantly although they are never actually seen to disintegrate. Very few psychic investigators seem to be aware of this phenomenon, although my colleague Raymond Bayless and the late Hereward Carrington, the doyen of psychic investigators, were aware and made note of it.

Bayless' interest was due in part to a personal confrontation with an instantaneous disappearance. Several years after, he reported to me:

The Mystery of Teleportation

The event occurred in the summer of 1957. I am an artist by profession and was instructing one of my students at the time. The room was bare but for an easel and two four-legged stools. Other than this sparse furniture, the room was totally stark. Since the room had a large northern window, it was usually brilliantly lit. The floor was composed of linoleum tiles and was uncarpeted and rug-less.

I was just instructing my student about a fine point of painting. I was holding a long-handled Delta 2 brush. Accidentally the brush slipped from my hand and we both heard a loud "click" as it struck the floor. I reached down to pick it up . . . but it was gone! It had just vanished into thin air. Now, this is of course impossible. A brush cannot just disappear out of a bare room. But that is what happened. We both looked for it, but it had simply vanished. Remember, the only objects in the room were an easel and two stools and ourselves. The brush could not have been lost. Yet it apparently disappeared from the room after obviously striking the floor.

When I started a search throughout psychic history for similar cases, I found a body of them, but they seem very rare. It was Hereward Carrington who was the first to realize that these incidents are some form of psychic phenomenon; he wrote the only article on the "syndrome" ever to be published in a respectable parapsychological journal. Carrington's article, "Mysterious Disappearances," was appropriately subtitled "an informal discussion of a curious problem" and appeared in the December, 1930, issue of *Psychic Research*, which was then the official organ of the American Society for Psychical Research. In it, Carrington chronicled several secondhand cases, which had been reported to him over the years and which he had personally investigated by interviewing the witnesses. These cases were disturbingly similar to the one reported by Bayless. One case was reported by the famous magician Fred Keating, who at the time was with his aged grandmother in their apartment. The elderly woman was reading aloud to him as he reclined on a living room sofa. The cozy scene was suddenly interrupted by the ringing of the phone. The old woman put down the book, laid her glasses on it, and left the room to answer the phone. When the call was over and she returned to her reading, the glasses had disappeared. Keating had not stirred from his position on the sofa and had clearly seen his grandmother place her glasses on the book. Yet during the brief interlude the glasses had vanished, and a search of the entire apartment failed to uncover them.

Another incident was reported to Carrington by a friend, a noted surgeon. The surgeon and his wife had invited three guests to their home. There was no domestic help in the house that day. One guest, Carrie, took off her hat and placed it on the floor by her chair. Although she didn't move from her seat for the next hour, when she bent over to pick up the hat, she found it gone. Needless to say, it was never seen again.

As Carrington concluded about these cases:

> We cannot really, seriously, believe them; and yet there they are! I submit the record, with many misgivings. Perhaps some of our members will volunteer to join me in a nice, comfortable asylum?

Actually all three of the incidents I have recorded occurred in similar circumstances: in each case there was a comfortable social situation; the victims were distracted at the time; all had some interest in the paranormal. What caused the disappearances? And where did the objects go?

The Mount Glastonbury disappearances suggest that a physical area might be the generator of these disturbances. Certainly it is way beyond the laws of simple coincidence that so many people have vanished from this one small geographical location. Other areas, such as the famous Bermuda Triangle, are of course well known. I'm not going to say very much about the Triangle since so much has been written about it. In fact, during the last two years we have seen an absolute "Triangle mania," with over a dozen books appearing on the market. However, it is necessary to bring up the Bermuda Triangle to illustrate the point that it is not at all unique and that disappearances within this area are simply *one* element of the disappearance mystery. As is well known, the Bermuda Triangle (which really isn't a triangle at all) is an area off the coast of Florida, encompassing Bermuda, where over the years many planes, ships, and passengers have vanished without any trace.

When the submarine *Scorpion* disappeared in the Triangle area in 1968, a new wave of interest was touched off. It was Ivan T. Sanderson, however, who discovered that there were in fact six triangles! After mapping out historical reports of strange disappearances around the world, he discovered a total of six areas on the world's surface where there have been an overabundance of disappearing craft. The amazing discovery, however, was that the triangles are situated in groups of threes and are in the same general latitude. The first set consists of the Bermuda Triangle, an area around the lower Mediterranean, and a third locale off the coast of Japan; all three rest on the same latitude lines, 30–40° N. The second group of disappearance areas are similarly lozenge-shaped points off the coast of Australia, Africa, and South America, all at 30–40° S.! When Sanderson first publicized his findings in the August, 1968, issue of *Argosy*, few took note. But now his discovery is much better known; the actual positioning of these areas has helped to demythologize the disappearances. The consistent pattern of these oceanic areas points to the fact that there might be a physical, albeit unnatural, explanation for the disappearances. But what is it? The explanations offered over the years have often been ridiculously extravagant. The three theories I hear most often are that craft are being abducted by UFOs, are being destroyed by an antimatter machine from the lost continent of Atlantis, or are falling through holes in space. Remember what I said earlier about not promulgating theories unless they can be tested or substantiated?

The phenomenon of strange disappearances is much more complicated than it is often believed to be. Let us recap the types of disappearances that have been noted so far:

1. For no apparent reason, people just vanish off the face of the earth and are never seen again.

2. Objects sometimes vanish in a similar fashion.

3. There are certain areas of the globe that are specifically cursed by disappearances.

The next question to be asked is simply, do vanished objects ever show up later? And if so, where were they during the interim? The answer to the first question is yes; in fact, vanished people sometimes show up as well. I will go into the second question shortly.

In 1930, Hereward Carrington investigated a case of a missing object that reappeared. A friend of his had the habit of leaving her keys on the dining room table. When she went to get them one day, she found they had vanished, and she had to have a duplicate set made. Several days later, the keys reappeared. The woman found the keys lying in a special tin box that was kept in the hallway. She was dumbfounded since she rarely opened this box, perhaps not more than a few times a year.

The fact that objects vanish and then reappear is an old psychic mystery which rests on better evidence than most people would think. William Blatty, the well-known author of *The Exorcist*, encountered this phenomenon following his mother's death. She was buried with a pendant around her neck; several months later, the very same medallion suddenly appeared around Blatty's neck!

More recently, there have been reports from South Africa about a woman around whom objects seem to appear and disappear inexplicably. At the First South African Conference of Parapsychology held in Johannesburg in October, 1973, L. H. van Loon, a consultant civil and structural engineer in Durban, reported several instances connected with his wife. Here is one example he reported and personally witnessed:

> ... a valuable brooch had mysteriously vanished from her locked jewel box. It was a particularly beautiful piece left to her by her grandmother whilst she was still a child in Burma. It occurred to her then that the brooch had not been simply stolen but had, in effect, been "spirited away" and that, given the right psychokinetic triggers, it could be summoned back. Her sentimental attachment to the brooch and a real annoyance at some psychic trick having been played on her undoubtedly put her in the right mood to attempt to bring about the recovery. Naturally, a description of her frame of mind, at the crucial moment of commanding the return of the brooch, must remain inadequate. One can only say that she appears to have visualized the brooch with great intensity and mentally seized control over intrisically related psychic elements which were then willfully directed to rematerialize the brooch in a most extraordinary manner. Some two or three days after the brooch's disappearance, she went to her cupboard to fetch a new pair of stockings which were still enclosed in the sealed packet in which they were purchased. Her brooch was inside the unopened packet, the pin stuck several times through the stocking material and firmly engaged in the catch.

As I said in the introduction, we really have to be hardheaded when evaluating reports like this. Having been a psychic investigator for a number of years, it has been my all too unpleasant duty to pick holes in such cases, show their weakness and the possibilities of fraud. The above case is

The Mystery of Teleportation

very weak for several reasons. First, Mrs. van Loon was practically the only witness. Apparently she was the one who "discovered" the missing jewelry; her husband does not make clear whether or not he saw the packet with the jewel in it or whether the facts were merely reported to him by his wife. Even if van Loon had seen the packet, there is little doubt that his wife could very easily have staged the whole incident. Carefully reading van Loon's presentation, "Some Unusual Psychokinetic Phenomena Associated with the Recovery of Lost Objects," I became more than frustrated over the poor evidence and even the worse reporting of it. Usually only Mrs. van Loon witnessed the recoveries and normally could have been responsible for the incidents. However, one report did attract my attention. During a visit by Mr. van Loon's parents, his mother's corset disappeared. A thorough search failed to recover it. It was later found in a closet of the elder van Loons' home in an entirely different city. Unfortunately all the van Loons were present at the time of discovery, and the report leaves open to question whether or not Mrs. van Loon, in a moment when the family was distracted, could have placed the corset in the closet herself.

Although the evidence is weak, van Loon ended his presentation with four conclusions about these incidents: first, that his wife believes she has the psychic ability to willfully cause objects to disappear and reappear. Second, sometimes objects disappear spontaneously due to what he calls "psychic trickery," but these instances are probably linked to his wife's abilities. Third, in some cases, objects that appear to have been stolen reappear nonetheless. Finally, objects reappear in odd places or under odd circumstances, as though some intelligence were trying to prove the supernaturalness of the whole business.

What is one to think of the van Loon affair? One can certainly be skeptical yet undoubtedly intrigued at the same time. The only way to resolve the issue would be to test Mrs. van Loon under controlled conditions. This approach was used with an enigmatic man named T. Lynn over fifty years ago. Like Mrs. van Loon, Lynn also felt he could make objects appear in his presence. A series of controlled and photographically monitored tests were carried out with him in the 1920s by the British College of Psychic Science and by its research officer, Colonel Mowbray. For these tests, Lynn would first disrobe and allow himself to be searched completely. This included searching his hair, all body orifices and other places that an object could be secreted. He was then redressed by the experimenters and placed into a shirt and pair of trousers *they* had brought, and put inside a large sack, with only his head protruding. The lights were lowered, and soon small objects would drop in front of him. These consisted of lumps of coal, shells, and other rather mundane material.

Of course, the first questions that come to mind are, could Lynn have had an accomplice among the experimenters, or could he have outwitted the controls? The rather amazing photographs taken by Mowbray do not support either of these arguments. Mowbray was able to procure several excellent photographs of the objects hovering in front of Lynn, often connected to him by a tiny ray of light. All of the experimenters and Lynn himself are in their proper places, and Lynn is still completely encased in the sack. Lynn was later brought to London to be tested at the college's own laboratory, with similar results.

Unfortunately, evidence that material objects do disappear and then reappear later rarely rests on such controlled conditions. But I have found one extremely well-documented case observed by two witnesses. The witnesses were my colleague Raymond Bayless and our mutual friend, Attila (Art) von Szalay, a rather extraordinary psychic with whom I've shared many psychic adventures.* As Bayless reported to me:

> Mr. von Szalay and I were walking down Hollywood Boulevard one afternoon in 1957 when we decided to visit a leather goods store which faced onto the boulevard. Mr. von Szalay was talking to the proprietor when I noticed an odd Canadian penny lying on his desk. I was intrigued by the coin—it had a picture of one of England's princesses on it and I had never seen one like it—so I picked it up and took a closer look at it. I noticed that one side of the coin had a short scratch across it. (Since the coin was lost some years later I cannot check its date.) I was so interested in the coin that I offered to buy it from the shop proprietor, but he declined my offer. Naturally I was disappointed. As Mr. von Szalay and I left the store, I looked back toward the proprietor and his desk. As we left the store to walk down the boulevard, I glanced back a final time and saw the coin still sitting on the desk. I regretted once more that I had not been able to buy it.
>
> We had walked only about a hundred feet down the block

---

* For a complete report on Mr. von Szalay, see my previous book, *In Search of the Unknown* (New York: Taplinger, 1976).

The Mystery of Teleportation

when, suddenly, I distinctly felt a small object hit me on the elbow and then fall against my pant leg. I looked down immediately. There, on the sidewalk, and at my feet, lay the same penny I had seen in the shop. I made sure by checking the scratch on the one side. It was the same coin!

Needless to say, Mr. von Szalay was just as surprised as I was. He too examined the coin and agreed with me that—inasmuch as we had seen the coin last on the proprietor's desk—there was no way that the coin could have been transported normally.

I have spent considerable time discussing cases of objects popping in and out of space in order to set the stage for the next step in my presentation. If it is possible for objects to disappear, travel lengthy distances, and then reappear, could not *people* pop in and out of space as well?

The transportation of the human body is not only given some inherent credibility by cases of mysterious disappearances, but also by a long tradition in our culture concerning people who disappear from one place and turn up, usually dazed, someplace else. Usually they feel that they have been transported by some superhuman agency. There are cases recorded in the Bible, there are medieval reports of people being borne away by fairies and turning up miles away, and there are cases recorded during séances and during poltergeist outbreaks. Only recently, Dr. Jacques Vallee, the well-known UFO expert and scientist, wrote in his book *Passport to Magonia* that these legends are suspiciously similar to the reports of UFO abductions that hit the press every so often. Could we be dealing with a real phenomenon? I think this is an actual possibility.

One of the most sensational of these reports was recorded by Dr. Joseph Lapponi in 1906. Lapponi, a Roman Catholic physician attached to the Vatican, was especially charged to investigate spiritualism. During the course of his investigations, he was confronted by the bizarre transportation of Alfred and Paul Pansini, who on several occasions would simply vanish and then shortly afterward appear miles away. An official report, *Ipnotismo e Spiritismo*, was made by Lapponi on his investigations into the occult, and in it he included the case of the Pansini brothers. The boys were eight and ten years old, respectively. A few of their disappearances follow: in one half hour they disappeared from Ruvo and reappeared on a boat at sea near Barletta; during a ten-minute period they vanished from an open square in Ruvo and were discovered in Trani.

These reports might seem ridiculous, preposterous, and either obvious hoaxes or fabrications. I certainly would share in the skepticism had not at least one of their flights been witnessed by an outside investigator. The investigator, Bishop Bernardi, had carefully sealed the house, but, while discussing their disappearances with Mrs. Pansini, he suddenly found that the children were gone.

Lapponi later traced down an almost identical case again involving two brothers who would vanish and then reappear far away, having traversed several miles in an incredibly short span of time.

The natural explanation for these flights is fraud. But *if the accounts are correctly written*, and this is a very important point, then the children were recorded to have disappeared and reappeared within too short a time to have traveled to their destinations in any normal way.

As Vallee and others have indicated, the mysterious and supernatural transportation of the human body has its roots in an old tradition. The Pansini brothers are not unique in this respect. For example, Robert Kirk in his 1692 book, *The Secret Commonwealth of Elves, Fauns, and Fairies*, reports several cases of people who disappeared and reappeared later in a different locale. Sometimes there were good witnesses to the escapades. Kirk wrote of one unfortunate man:

> His neibours often perceaved this man to disappear at a certane Place, and about one Hour after to become visible, and discover himselfe near a Bow-shot from the first Place. It was in that Place where he became invisible, said he, that the Subterraneans [elves] did encounter and combate with him.

During spiritualism's heyday, there were many nonsensical tales of mediums being dematerialized from the séance room, but the phenomenon hit the presses once again in 1965 when the strange story of Cornelio Closa, Jr. was picked up, not only by the Philippine press, but by UPI as well. Although separated by over a hundred years, "the disappearing boy of Manila" is almost identical to the Pansini brothers. In addition, the case is supported by at least some halfway decent evidence. (The use of historic parallel is an important point and one I use in my work and shall use in this book. If I come across something odd and out of place, even for the paranormal, I get suspicious. But when I come across two or more oddities that appear to be identical occurrences, separated by many years or in different cultures, this signals a pattern. Patterns are almost as important as corroborative evidence and, when they are uncovered, represent at least *one* point in favor of the chronicles—no matter how bizarre— being more likely.)

The Closa case first broke in 1953 and the victim, Cornelio Closa, Jr., even today maintains the absolute truth of his mysterious encounters, as do those witnesses still living, including his father and the American clergyman Lester Sumrall. Now a married man with several children, Closa is reticent about discussing his experiences but did give a UPI interview in 1965 to Vicente Maliwang. Closa comes across as anything but a mystic. A clean-shaven family man, he lives comfortably on the income he earns as an electrician. He knows his story is more bizarre than the usual tales told about psychic encounters.

"Since it happened," Closa told reporters, "I have been reluctant to talk about it to strangers. In this world of jet planes and spaceships, who will believe it? If you tell me the same story, I won't believe you and I'll just laugh in your face." Eyeing his young family and motioning to his wife to take the children out to play, Closa added, "My wife knows the story but we don't talk about it anymore. She understands, but the children won't."

Now for the story itself! The account begins at the elementary school Cornelio attended when he was twelve years old. He was not a model student by any means. He enjoyed skipping classes, prefered playing to classwork, and generally described himself as "naughty."

One day Cornelio met a rather mysterious girl about his own age and dressed in white; she motioned to him to follow her as she touched him gently on his hand. Cornelio described his next sensations as like those in a dream world. This same encounter occurred several times.

Let me stop here and say that there is nothing too unusual about this type of encounter taken by itself. This may shock the reader, but it shouldn't. When I studied abnormal psychology, I was surprised to note how many otherwise normal people hallucinate phantom friends under certain conditions of stress. Loneliness is often the cause among children, and many parents have noted that their offspring consort with "invisible" playmates. But adults have these envisionings too, and often for the same reason. Intense isolation or loneliness can cause the mind to create imaginary but very real companions. Stories of these "encounters" have come to us from prisoners in isolation cells and also from explorers. Admiral Byrd, during his hellish explorations of the world's most desolate areas, wrote about the mysterious people who became his companions, and he noted their appearances in his diaries. Cornelio strikes the reader as a disturbed, shy boy, so his encounters with the lovely girl seem more a psychological experience than a psychic one.

During the period of his meetings with the girl, Cornelio started to undergo strange disappearances. Unfortunately, this testimony comes strictly from Cornelio. He told reporters that he would simply vanish off the street, even from his classroom and sometimes in front of witnesses. Finally, in desperation, the family locked him in the house, but he continued to disappear in spite of it. The family, left with little recourse, took the boy to a mental institution for psychiatric testing. He was declared normal but was placed in a juvenile delinquency institution before the authorities convinced his parents that the lad was better off at home. During the sequence of events, the strange disappearances stopped. So did the appearances of the girl.

Seeing that he would have to "spill the beans," so to speak, about his disappearances, he finally told his father about the phantom girl. She was now appearing again, and when she came, Cornelio disappeared! Cornelio's father searched out anyone who could help. Neighbors, spiritualists, and clergymen were all consulted.

By March, 1952, the "disappearing boy of Manila" had gotten so much notoriety that a retired Navy man and now clergyman, Reverend Roman Quisol, came to investigate. He in turn advised the Closas to consult an American pastor, Reverend Lester Sumrall. Sumrall diagnosed diabolic infestation, and after a series of mini-exorcisms, the disappearances stopped. Sumrall himself met with reporters in 1965 and testified to the mysterious transports and to the accuracy of the boy's accounts.

Evidentially speaking, this case is rather weak. There were few witnesses to it or at least few who could be traced, the boy was noted for playing hooky, and no attention was paid in the interview to just what precautions the family took to lock Cornelio in. And never underestimate a young boy's ability to escape from a locked house! On the other hand, these disappearances were frequent and apparently so impressive that several ministers were convinced of their authenticity.

Actually, there are on record even more spectacular cases than *these* disappearing children. Keel, in his *Our Haunted Planet*, has tracked down cases of ostensible teleportation over even more extraordinary distances than those of the Pansini brothers. A Londoner is reported to have found himself in South Africa, a Cleveland girl awakened in Australia, etc. The cases go back for centuries. One of the earliest comes from 1593 (October 24 to be exact) when a soldier from Manila found himself in Mexico City!

Actually many of these cases, when not pure fiction, could easily be due to normal causes. In many cases, people with amnesia disappear and reappear in distant cities, which strongly suggests that they were victims of what in abnormal psychology is called *fugue states*. A person just gives up his own personality (usually under mental stress), leaves his home, and suddenly finds himself living or staying in a different city with no memory of how he got there or how long he has been there. Under hypnosis, his memories often can be traced. Other cases are not so easily explained. Mysterious disappearances, like the Vermont cases, come in cycles or are localized in one geographic area. In other cases, the victims do reappear days later, suddenly finding themselves wandering about city streets.

But back to Manila's disappearing boy. If you were to ask me point-blank whether I believe Cornelio's account, I couldn't give a firm answer. I could only remind the reader what I said in the introduction to this book: the wilder the claim, the higher the probability of its being false.

Why, then, have I even quoted a case that admittedly must be questionable at best and dubious at worst? Despite my great reservations, the case still intrigues me, not so much because of the account itself, but because of its similarity to older accounts of the same phenomenon noted by the Vatican in the early 1900s. In each case, the children involved were at the age of puberty; they disappeared from home and were found miles away, and to all evidence they seemed to be unhappy.

These characteristics are all very typical of the poltergeist. As is well known, a poltergeist is a phenomenon that plagues families by throwing objects about their houses. These rampages very often center on a child in his or her teens, and the force seems to be a way for the child, or focus person, to use psychokinesis unconsciously to vent repressed hostilities and emotions. One of the poltergeist's favorite tricks is to make objects disappear. The objects will sometimes later reappear (for example, shoplifted shoes reappearing in the store) or will just fall into the room from the ceiling. In one case investigated by Professor Hans Bender of Freiburg University, a woman was besieged by tools which fell all over her room during the poltergeist infestation. The woman picked up all the objects, placed them in a box, and sat on it! Nonetheless, objects still disappeared from the box and fell back into the room. During another case also investigated by Bender, witnesses and family members outside the house watched as objects placed inside appeared by the roof and fell slowly in a zig-zag motion to the ground outside. These incidents do give the concept of "matter-through-matter" credibility.

It is my own belief that *if* these accounts of mysterious transportations of objects and the human body are genuine, they represent some form of poltergeist activity. In very rare cases, human transportation is noted in poltergeist cases; poltergeist attacks are also mentioned in the biographies of some of the saints, who encountered this phenomenon.* For example, in the sinister witchcraft manual, *Malleus Maleficarum*, used during the notorious witch craze in Europe, it is written that "Vincent of Beauvais . . . related a story told by S. Peter Damian of a five-year-old son of a nobleman, who was for the time living in a monastery, and one night he was carried out of the monastery into a locked mill, where he was found in the morning." The boy was apparently the focus of a poltergeist, and like Cornelio, he underwent several fantasy-like experiences during the transportation.

In 1883, a poltergeist case erupted in England in the home of a Dr. MacDonald (this name is a fictitious one to protect the identity of a well-known physician and his wife). The case was witnessed by the couple as well as by their neighbors, the Thompsons. The poltergeist apparently focused on their maid, Bridget, who was fired soon afterward and took employment with another local family. At first, household items would vanish from sight some never to be seen again. Then the poltergeist started attacking people. When objects

* Refer, for example, to Raymond Bayless' *The Enigma of the Poltergeist* (West Nyack, N.Y.: Parker, 1967), Chapter 20, "Saints and Poltergeists."

did reappear, they usually materialized around the ceiling and floated to the floor. The apported objects were generally warm to the touch, a very typical trait in poltergeist cases. As we have noted, poltergeists usually center on one individual in the house, and he or she becomes the brunt of the attacks. This was certainly true of the case reported in *Occult Review* (Vol. VI, pp. 330-1) by Inkster Gilbertson, who was acquainted with it:

> So sensitive did the maid Bridget become to the influences about the house that she was in a state of trance every day—frequently all day. Sometimes she would disappear mysteriously, and after absent for hours, would return as mysteriously as she disappeared. This became so troublesome that at last her mistress had to send her away ...
>
> A few days after she had gone, [as recorded by Mrs. MacDonald on March 20, 1895] the most appalling thing happened. At seven o'clock in the evening, the Thompsons were assembled in the kitchen, for they were now without a maid, when the door burst suddenly open, and in tumbled Bridget helplessly on the floor. She was without hat or jacket or boots, and wore her ordinary house shoes—which bore no trace of travel—and a rough apron, as if she had been at work.

According to this rather wild account, Bridget remained in a trance for several hours. When she came to, she seemed to have amnesia and spoke disjointedly about having gone to "fairyland." Note here *again* that the victim tells of having been transported through fantasy-type realms. The MacDonalds contacted the maid's new employers who testified that the girl *had* vanished from their house shortly after having been seen cleaning boots. While the MacDonalds were questioning Bridget, more objects fell into the room in typical poltergeist fashion.

This transportation phenomenon has also been recorded in connection with mystics, as in the case of Angelica Darocca, the blood-sweating girl of Tyrol. An intense ascetic who manifested the "stigmata," the appearance of blood or wounds on the hands, feet, head, or side where Christ was wounded, Angelica often disappeared from her cell only to reappear there later. During these disappearances, apparitions of her were seen in neighboring cities.

The human body is not the only living object that has been transported during poltergeist manifestations. In his book on bizarre poltergeist behavior, *Mind Over Space* (which I have drawn upon often in this chapter), the Hungarian expert Dr. Nandor Fodor reported an extraordinary case of teleportation that occurred in Italy in 1936.

> Phenomena of incendiary infestation have been recently established on a farm in Prignano (Salerno): fires broke out spontaneously, destroyed household objects, and burnt persons and animals. Bricks and stones fell in the rooms, although the windows were closed. There was spontaneous displacement of objects. *A pair of oxen were even found to have been carried from one stall to another without human agency.* The *carabinieri*, assisted by young fascists and other local persons, after long and careful observation came to the conclusion that it was impossible for anyone to play a bad joke. An anonymous Neapolitan doctor and psychical researcher who was on the spot found a sixteen-year-old girl with strong mediumistic faculties who was the involuntary means of the striking phenomena.

Of course during the heyday of mediums and séances, the reported teleportation of the medium's body was commonplace. But most of these accounts are easily attributed to fraud. Usually the medium would be found outside a sealed cage or outside the séance room. Reading the accounts today it does not seem at all unlikely that a spare key or pick was used to make the escape in order to defraud the startled sitters. But there is one case of human teleportation that just can't be explained away. This is the case of the Marquis Carlo Centurione Scotto. Although Fodor quotes the account in his book *Mind Over Space*, a much more complete and impressive account appears in Gwendolyn Hack's *Modern Psychic Mysteries* which offers full documentation of the Marquis' Millesimo Castle experiments.

The Marquis had traveled to England in the hope of finding a medium through whom he could contact his dead son. He felt he had succeeded in George Valiantine, a famous medium of the 1920s. When Scotto returned home, he set up what is called a "home circle" in an attempt to precipitate psychic manifestations. Home circles, which were very popular during this era, consisted of a group of good friends who would get together and sit in the dark, week after week, invoking the help of "spirit entities" to come and produce psychic phenomena. Although the rules were somewhat complicated, the basic premise was that if conditions were suitable, eventually *physical* phenomena would occur within the group.

The Mystery of Teleportation 25

Most common among these effects were rapping noises, "touches," breezes, odors, and finally the movement or levitation of objects.

It is surprising how often these experiments work. I helped organize such a circle among friends in 1968, and over a period of weeks we gradually achieved some results. At the present time, a group in Canada headed by A. R. G. Owen, a former Cambridge geneticist, has also achieved impressive results.

Scotto was no less successful, and his circle eventually produced apports (teleported objects falling into the room like those reported in connection with the medium T. Lynn), independent voices, etc. The climax of the experiments was the alleged teleportation of the Marquis' body out of the castle. This account is, to my knowledge and belief, one of the best reported and documented, if not the only decently substantiated, transportation of the human body in psychic history.

The remarkable séance was held on July 29, 1928. Among the experimenters were his always present friends the Rossis, Gwendolyn Kelly Hack, and the famous Italian psychic investigator and scholar Ernesto Bozzano.

The séance began at 10:45 P.M. After the lights had been lowered, breezes enveloped the room, a table was dragged about by some unknown force, a speaking trumpet flew into the air, and voices filled the room. While these manifestations were in progress, the sitters quickly noted their observations to each other, and the Marquis was frequently heard to report that he had not moved from his chair. Suddenly he cried out, "I can no longer feel my legs." *Immediately* after this odd remark quiet reigned, and then an animated discussion broke out. It is possible to reconstruct the exact words from a transcript of the séance made at the time by Hack:

Mme. Rossi spoke out: "I feel as though something extraordinary were happening. I feel around me an indefinable vacuum which is very alarming."

The Marquise was frightened and shouted to her husband, "Carlo! Carlo!"

Another sitter, M. Castellani, tried to avert alarm and quickly and intelligently retorted, "Hush, the medium has fallen into a trance. Keep quiet. Don't move ... M. Carlo, M. Carlo! No answer." Castellani instructed Mme. Rossi: "Stretch out your hand to feel what position the medium is in."

And then the shock came—he was gone! Although the

room was dark, the Rossis crouched on the floor feeling about for Scotto. Since the Marquis was still missing, Bozzano ordered the séance ended and the room lit. Indeed the Marquis had vanished from the *locked* room.

A frantic search began. The castle was covered room by room, then the stables. The circle was in despair. Mrs. Hack, however, was versed in automatic writing, and through her came words of consolation advising the sitters that the Marquis was quite all right and was being guarded as he slept.

Ultimately the Marquis was found—fast asleep—in a locked granary. Castellani woke Scotto, who was at first frightened and disoriented. He couldn't fathom why he was in the granary. Afraid that he was going mad, he burst into sobs. Castellani tried to assure the Marquis that he had only drunk a little too much wine that evening and had fallen asleep. But the Marquis knew better. It might be noted that a few months later Scotto gave up the sittings altogether.

It should be remembered that, according to the detailed notes taken at the time, right after Scotto's words, "I can no longer feel my legs," absolute quiet enveloped the room, so Scotto could not have escaped the locked room—in complete darkness—without making some noise. Furthermore, there were present at the séance several people who were good observers, as indicated by the intelligent and detailed notes of the séance. A diagram of the séance room in the Hack book also substantiates the virtual impossibility of the Marquis escaping undetected. The room was small, and the window and door to it were far from where Scotto sat during the séances. He would have to have knocked into someone or something on his way out. Hack and Bozzano contributed several pages to an analysis of the incident, including counter-hypotheses and cross-examination of the witnesses.

It was a great satisfaction to me to meet someone in 1972 who actually had known Carlo Centurione Scotto, although only briefly. This was no less than Dr. Emilio Servadio, one of Italy's leading psychoanalysts who is also deeply interested in parapsychology. He had met Scotto only once and had found him a rather pompous, dogmatic man. But when I asked him about the Millesimo Castle experiments, Dr. Servadio had to admit that, while he felt that the Rossis were faking a great deal during the experiments, it could not be denied that many mysterious events really did take place.

The Carlo Centurione Scotto case, much as I have abbreviated it, establishes that the human body can be transported

The Mystery of Teleportation

from one place to another by psychic means. But let's go on to another enigma.

We have pretty well established that people and objects disappear into nowhere, or show up out of nowhere, or disappear and then reappear sometime later. All this is reminiscent of the U.S. postal system: letters never arrive, show up weeks after they were mailed, or undergo similar remarkable adventures. This analogy isn't meant to be totally flippant. What I'm suggesting is that all of these oddities represent a *transportation system*. And like any other system, things are bound to go wrong every once in a while!

The concept of instantly transporting objects and people via teleportation through some sort of "hyper-dimension" is certainly not mere science fiction. Strange disappearances and psychic phenomena indicate the reality of apportation, and it is a concept that has intrigued scientists and world governments alike.

There are a number of people who have some acquaintance with our field and who come up with intriguing though totally irrational delusions that our military and government are secretly conducting experiments into the paranormal or are nefariously covering up strange discoveries. I'm not what one would call a paranoid-tripper, but my skepticism did become a little shaky as the result of an encounter reported with relish by Ivan Sanderson. Sanderson was once talking to Pentagon officials about UFOs, as part of a regular briefing session. Although the conversation was not top secret, it was obviously confidential. Sanderson, who was always a gutsy sort of person, decided to stretch the conversation as far as he could and asked the officials if he could talk to any scientists experimenting with "teleportation." Why he thought such experiments were going on is somewhat of a mystery itself, but even he was shocked at the response; all hell broke loose. One top official screamed, "We don't mention that subject." He asserted that he didn't know anything about it, yet another official paradoxically concluded, "Anyhow, we don't call it teleportation any more; we call it ITF." For the uninitiated, ITF stands for instantaneous transference. So obviously something was up!

As I said, in any transportation system, things are bound to get fouled up. Just as letters never arrive or get delivered to the wrong address, we might expect that teleported objects sometimes get lost too. They might never show up at all, or they might just appear in ridiculous places at totally incongruous times. So, if everything I've reported is true, you would expect material objects to be found in odd places, or they might just drop out of the clear blue sky. Maybe I'm being a little post-hoc, but of course just this type of thing has been happening for years. These occurrences are a delight to Forteans (remember Charles Fort who started cataloguing these events?) while being a royal pain in the ——— to conventional scientists. They can be classified under two general headings: (1) mysterious rainfalls and (2) articles found in "impossible" places.

Not very much need be said about mysterious falls of bizarre matter. Charles Fort began collecting news accounts of them years ago, and every year several of them make backpage stories in the world's press. At various times, various geographic areas have been the sites of rains of peas, beans, flesh and blood (!), fish, frogs, metal cylinders, mysterious strandlike substances called "angel hair," and everything else conceivable.

Although these falls have been recorded for centuries, they came to national prominence in 1947 when biologist A. D. Bajkov reported eyewitnessing one of these phenomena in Marksville, Louisiana, when he was carrying out field investigations for the Department of Wild Life and Fisheries. The scientist reported the deluge to *Science* (April 22, 1949), this country's leading—and most conservative—scientific journal. For one hour, fish fell from the sky. Hundreds of fish, all species indigenous to the area, fell all over the town. (In some cases, only one species of animal may fall and sometimes that species is either rare or not indigenous.) Rock falls have also been reported, and there was once a rain of peas and beans near Los Angeles.

Scientists have no explanation for these falls and usually prefer to ignore them. One common augument is that they are by-products of freak tornado activity which has picked up the specimens and redeposited them. This theory is not only shallow, it is preposterous. Objects are often *selectively* deposited, as when a specific variety of life rains down, for example, a rare or uncommon genus of frog or fish. Current theories cannot explain falls of such things as blood and flesh—perhaps the most grisly of all; such a rainfall of meat and blood occurred in Sao Paulo, Brazil, in 1968.

Forteans and scientists alike have long hoped that a normal physical explanation would eventually solve the puzzle, but I doubt if one will ever turn up. For some reason, Forteans are not very knowledgeable about psychic phenomena. This may seem strange, but it is true. In fact, Ivan Sanderson almost had a horror of them. In any event, mysterious rainfalls are often reported in poltergeist cases. As we explained earlier, the poltergeist is produced by a great upheaval of psychic energy within a family generally caused by one or more members of the group. One of the most common poltergeist manifestations is rock-pelting. Rocks may literally bombard the outside and inside of the house. This parallel suggests that these Fortean falls do not have a physical basis at all but may be a form of psychic or poltergeist activity. But more about that later.

Before leaving this topic, we should note the strange array of "sky junk" that has been falling from the heavens for years. Huge pieces of metal or other foreign matter, including such things as heavy hardware or metal sheets, sometimes just plop down out of clear, unclouded, and uninhabited (by planes, that is) skies. Needless to say, "sky junk" cases were on record before there was any sort of man-made aircraft. One of the most common explanations for both sky junk and the strange rainfalls is the UFO refuse theory which proposes that all these objects are excess baggage or purpose-already-served material that the UFO-nauts are ready to dispose of. I don't buy that explanation, and I'll show why later.

Even if we could sit back and assure ourselves that all these aerial phenomena are quite normal, we still would have to put up with what some Forteans called OOPARTS, meaning *out of place artifacts*. Every so often, artifacts are found within other matter in totally impossible ways. Some years ago there was a great deal of publicity about a perfectly formed bird embryo that was found inside a pitless peach! That case, however, could easily have been a hoax.

A more exemplary illustration of an OOPART was the discovery of steel nails in a Scottish sandstone quarry embedded in rock centuries older than steel itself. Odd objects, including relatively modern coins and jewelry, have similarly been found in ancient coal deposits with no explanation as to how they could possibly have gotten there.

Ivan Sanderson came up with three explanations for OOPARTS: (1) that before man, another technologically advanced civilization controlled the earth,* (2) that they are forms of dematerialized, teleported, and rematerialized objects; (3) that these objects are remnants of ancient extraterrestrial visitors.

Sanderson easily disposed of hypothesis (1) on the basis of its inherent improbability. But he never tried to argue the pros and cons of hypothesis (2) or (3). Of course, with the von Daniken craze going full blast, the ancient astronaut theory is gaining widespread support, but I don't like that theory either.

The apportation or teleportation of objects is an old psychic manifestation and we have seen how it occurs spontaneously during poltergeist attacks and how it can be induced by gifted psychics such as T. Lynn. What of objects that vanish during poltergeist outbreaks and are never found again? Are they deposited elsewhere? To return to the U.S. postal service analogy, OOPARTS are letters that just missed their mark.

I think that much of what we call Fortean phenomena will ultimately be found to have a psychic basis. For this reason, mysterious disappearances and reappearances are probably a variant of the same force that scientists have witnessed in the course of matter-through-matter transportation during, say, poltergeist attacks.

Rock falls, flesh falls, OOPARTS, and their ilk seem to me to probably be teleported matter—not UFOs, not ancient civilizations, not even hoaxers. All the other theories are based on rather extravagant post-hoc evidence. They are unnecessary and go beyond anything the bare facts would allow us to work with. As I will show later, *many* UFOs (but not all) are probably a form of psychic manifestation.

So now we get to the really big question: Where do these things go between the time they vanish and the time they (hopefully) reappear. This leads back to the concept of parallel universes, multiple universes, or what I call "hyper-dimensions." This is not the same old science-fiction nonsense about the fourth dimension but a scientifically valid concept that other universes might intertwine with our own. This is hardly a new theory at all. There is physical as well as mathematical evidence that hyper-dimensions exist, but it would get unduly technical to do into this. Actually, the number of parallel universes could be almost infinite.

Could objects or people get caught in these multiple uni-

---

* You can also call this the Keel hypothesis since John Keel has been its most noted modern supporter (see his *Our Haunted Planet*).

verses—sliding out of our world and into the next? Strange human disappearances are rather like tornados. If one turns up (or out!) another is likely to follow. All students of strange disappearances have noted their cyclic nature. They come in actual epidemics. Simultaneous disappearances of children occurred in Ireland and in Belgium in August, 1869, and other outbreaks can be cited. These disappearances are often geographically linked, indicating some type of momentary interface between hyper-dimensions and our own world.

And then there are the parallel cases of Oliver Larch of Indiana in 1889 and David Lang of Tennessee in 1880. In both cases, the victims walked out of their homes and just vanished seconds later. In both cases, their voices were heard calling for help. And in both cases, although their voices were heard, their bodies were nowhere to be found. The voices were just disembodied entities pleading for help. Both men disappeared in totally open areas, and they were never seen or heard from again.

Did one case plagiarize from the other? Or were they just fanciful tales?

To repeat once again: the wilder the claim, the less its inherent probability. But can we dismiss all of them? To quote another time-worn maxim, where there's smoke, there's fire. No matter how bizarre our accounts of unworldly events get, they often do follow patterns. From teleporting brothers to OOPARTS, these enigmas have confronted man in many different ages and in many different lands. Strange things are happening on our planet, and ignoring them will not remedy the situation. Sticking our heads in the sands of three-dimensional reality cannot hide the mysteries we must eventually confront. We cannot escape from the cosmic interface. I do not know how *much* of the material I have presented here would turn out to be due to preternatural causes were we able to consult some omniscient being, but I am sure much of it would. The ability of matter to transport itself from one place to another, not through but beyond space, is certainly a reality, or, if you like, a metareality. It really would not matter if it were only a copper penny teleported from one room to the next during a poltergeist invasion, or a legion of British soldiers transported to Alaska. In any case, a startling and horrendous phenomenon is manifest which science must confront. It was for this reason that Charles Fort loved to intimidate the scientific establishment with his news clippings, press releases, and tongue-in-cheek speculations. Hyper-dimensions of time and space are science's greatest challenge.

I ended my first chapter with a quote from Sanderson's *Uninvited Visitors*. I can't resist ending this one with another:

> To be truly open-minded you have got to have considerable experience of reality, a lot of training in scientific methodology, an almost all-embracing skepticism—especially of skeptics—and what can only be called a rather profoundly philosophical frame of mind. If you are going to follow the precepts of scientific inquiry, you have to be prepared to at least consider if not accept anything that you stumble across along the path. You just cannot stop short and say, "That's too much. I don't believe it." That it is too much for *you* is permissible, and for you to admit it is laudable, but to refuse to consider anything on the grounds that you don't believe it is, from a scientific point of view, inexcusable. The Age of Belief is over, and we are struggling to enter the Age of Reason, wherein facts alone count.

CHAPTER 3
Mysteries and Miracles

> A miracle is a violation of the laws of nature; and as a firm and unalterable experience has established these laws, the proof against a miracle, from the very nature of the fact, is as entire as any argument from experience can possible be imagined . . . no testimony is sufficient to establish a miracle, unless the testimony be of such a kind that its falsehood would be more miraculous than the fact which it endeavors to establish.

These are the immortal words of David Hume which appear in his eighteenth-century treatise, *An Enquiry Concerning Human Understanding*. But even today the concept behind these words exerts an armlock on the thinking of millions of people. Who among us would not prefer to believe that someone lied rather than believe that he witnessed a miracle? Shouts of "impossible," "unbelievable," or "delusion" have been the only rewards for those who have experienced the miraculous.

David Hume's words epitomize the rationalist mind and philosophy. And it is a comforting philosophy at that, since any phenomenon that disobeys natural law can merely be thrown out without consideration! Since miraculous events run counter to our everyday experience, of course they don't exist!

Although this matter-of-fact approach to daily life may appeal to most people, the simple fact remains that what we might call "miracles" are occurring every day. Now, miracles differ from psychic phenomena (which indicate that within man's mind are potentials such as ESP and psychokinesis that can transcend time and space). Miracles point to even more bizarre forces in the world, spiritual forces which might directly interact in our lives. In 1953, throngs of devotees huddled around a painting of the Madonna in Italy which had begun to cry very real tears. In 1958, hundreds of skeptics and believers alike watched a glowing apparition of the Madonna appear atop a church in Egypt. In Spain in 1962, onlookers watched as a teen-aged girl levitated off the ground while in religious ecstasy. These miracles have occurred during the last twenty-five years in Western culture. They demand an explanation. Are they spiritual wonders? Psychic phenomena? Or something even more complex ... another element of the cosmic interface?

Reverend Robert Lewis' first introduction to religion came from his Welsh-born Baptist grandmother, and he admitted with some embarrassment that she burst into tears of joy when he announced his intention to enter the ministry. As the years rolled by, Lewis threw himself into his canonical studies. It was his greatest regret that his grandmother died before the day of his ordination. He even told his friend, Reverend William Rauscher, that he wished she were alive so that he could watch her happiness when he told her that he had passed his ordination examinations. It was during this discussion, and in order to relax a bit, that Lewis walked over to his dresser to take off his tie. He took a quick look at his grandmother's photograph, which lay on the dresser, and shot an angry glance at Rauscher.

"Who's playing a joke? Who's been fooling around with my grandmother's picture?" he demanded.

Rauscher was shaken. He assured his friend that no one had entered the room while he had been there and then ...

> ... I went over to see what was troubling him. I was astounded! The photograph of Bob's grandmother was soaking wet, dripping, with a small pool of water spreading on the dresser under it.
>
> Examining the picture, we found that it was wet *inside* the glass. That was genuinely puzzling. The back of the picture, made of dyed imitation velvet, was so wet the velvet had streaked and faded.
>
> Removed from its frame, the photograph didn't dry quickly. When it did dry, the area about the face remained puffed, as though the water had originated there and run downward—from the eyes.

All through the annals of religion there have been stories of pictures that wept, statues that bled, Madonnas that cried, and icons that glowed with a warm radiance. Instances of these miracles have been reported from all over the globe. While very little has been written about these occurrences outside of religious tracts, they constitute a distinct classification of psychic phenomena. Nothing seems to create psychic manifestations of an unbelievable magnitude more than religious devotion or fervor. To me, Reverend Lewis' crying photograph was not a miracle but a form of psychic invasion. His grandmother often wept with joy, and Lewis, in order to recreate the event symbolically, used his telekinetic ability to create the miracle. We often use our psychic potential to carry out, albeit unconsciously, our secret desires and urges. Sometimes the unconscious projects our inner hostility and guilt, and a poltergeist is born. Occasionally the poltergeist will materialize pools of water in an infested house. During a recent outbreak in Germany, water mysteriously splashed about in one house, and subsequently neighboring houses were involved as well. Pools of water suddenly appeared on floors, rivers of water poured down staircases, and eventually the entire block of homes was affected.

Lewis underwent a mini-trauma when he passed his ordination exams. He wanted to share his joy with his first religious mentor; he wanted to see her cry with happiness, so he used his psychic ability to stage the event.

During the last few decades there has been almost an epidemic of weeping Madonnas both in the United States and in Europe. In each instance, onlookers have reported that water began to drip from, or even inundate, icons, paintings, or statues. The inexplicable appearance of liquid, often forming from the eyes of the figures, has led onlookers to believe that the figures were actually crying. Sometimes scientists have been brought in to investigate the phenomena. Here are a few reports that have come to us over the last twenty years.

Mrs. Anne Poore, a housewife from Philadelphia, Pennsylvania, was praying before a twenty-eight-inch-high plaster statue of Jesus. She was praying for the souls of those who, in our super-technological age, have been turning away from the Church. As she finished her silent meditation, she looked up at the benign face of the statue with its outstretched hands. "My heart stopped beating," Mrs. Poore admitted to reporters. "Two ruby-red drops of blood had appeared over the plaster wounds in its palms. I was terrified—I could see it was real blood."

Since 1974, hundreds of witnesses—the devout and skeptics alike—have watched the statue bleed. The blood appears on the palms and streams downward over the statue's arms, sometimes drenching the entire figure. The flows are reportedly most profuse on Fridays and Holy Days. In order to share her "miracle" with others, Mrs. Poore donated the figure to St. Luke's Episcopalian Church in Eddystone, Pennsylvania, a southern suburb of Philadelphia, where the statue has been studied by both ecclesiastic and scientific examiners as recently as 1976.

Father Chester Olszewski, pastor of St. Luke's, has been able to watch the blood flows on several occasions. He has examined the statue both during the periods of bleeding and when dry. Although guarded about the phenomenon, the priest is admittedly impressed by the manifestation and has told reporters: "Hundreds have come to my church to pray before the statue—and it has bled. Yet it stands on a shelf ten feet above the altar, where nobody can touch it. It has bled as long as four hours. I know there can be no trickery. Several times I've seen the palms dry—then minutes later have observed droplets of blood welling out of the wounds."

Even more amazing testimony about the statue comes from Dr. Joseph Rovito, a Philadelphia physician who has made a scientific examination of the figure. Rovito has X-rayed the plaster figure to see if any secret devices could have been walled into it to make it bleed. He found nothing suspicious. However, blood samples taken from the statue pose a curious problem. Although the flow would indicate that the figure is bleeding fresh blood, laboratory tests show the samples to be rather aged serum. While fresh blood would be expected to contain millions of red blood cells, the blood from the figure is extremely deficient in these cells, according to Dr. Rovito.

In a similar case, on March 16, 1960, a framed lithograph of the Virgin Mary began to shed tears in the home of Mrs. Pagona Catsounis in Island Park, New York. A local prelate, Reverend George Papadeas, told reporters, "When I arrived, a tear was drying beneath the left eye. Then just before the devotions ended, I saw another tear well in her left eye. It started as a small round globule of moisture in the corner of her left eye, and it slowly trickled down her face."

When the story reached the public, more than 4,000 penitents, miracle-mongers, and the curious paraded through the small apartment. The picture continued to weep for an entire week. After Reverend Papadeas blessed the house, the strange infestation stopped, and the picture itself was removed from the Catsounis home and enshrined at St. Paul's Greek Orthodox Church in Hempstead.

The Catsounis case had just been resolved when another picture began to weep in nearby Oceanside, New York. Father Papadeas was called in by Antonia Koulis, who was Mrs. Catsounis' aunt! Again, water streamed from the eyes of *her* glass-encased portrait. Archbishop Iakouos of the Greek Orthodox Church witnessed the miracle, and reporters, who were able to examine the picture immediately after the glass casing in which it was mounted was removed, found the back of the painting soaking wet. When the liquid was analyzed chemically, it was found not to be human tears. Later the Archbishop substituted another painting for the Koulis Madonna, and it too began to weep.

Unfortunately, the subsequent history of the Koulis icon makes it suspect. The figure was placed on display in Los Angeles at the Holy Transfiguration Russian Orthodox Church by Mrs. Koulis in 1964 where Los Angeles investigator Raymond Bayless made a visit to the church to see it firsthand. (Reproductions were placed on sale in order to collect money to erect a shrine to house the painting.) However the "tears" were hardly flowing—in fact, they were solid, and the Archbishop literally had to scrape off particles of the serum to give Bayless for analysis. Bayless noted that the substance tasted sweet, which alerted him to the fact that it was probably a sugar compound. There were two streams of serum from the eyes, but these were dry, with little evidence that anything had "flowed" to make the marks. A few solidified "tears" also dotted the face. Although many people claimed that the tears moved, Bayless was able to verify that the large solidified tears never budged from their position on the icon. He was able to make a closer examination of the portrait at a later date and discovered that the tear tracks were crystallized particles.

During the public viewing, people would often see the Madonna "cry," and large groups of people were taken in by the suggestion. One person would shout that a new tear was forming, and other visitors soon followed suit. Bayless witnessed one of these mirages but did not see any movement of the tears himself or any liquid flowing down the tracks. As he concluded:

> In the case of this weeping icon, it is my opinion that delusion, hysteria, or just poor powers of objective observation

> played a major part. Some viewers and worshippers were convinced they saw tears appear and move on the surface of the icon while my friend and I were present. On the other hand, we both were convinced, because of our careful examination, that the substance of the tear was not liquid and did not descend even a fraction of an inch ...

Conducting a postmortem on the Koulis Madonna a decade later, it is hard to dismiss the probability that the case was a hoax from the start, despite the impressive initial testimony from New York.

Rarely have proper investigations been made when these cases have hit the press or been reported to church officials. Dr. Nandor Fodor investigated a few cases in the United States which he included in his *Between Two Worlds* (from which the above cases were extracted). In Italy, Dr. Piero Cassoli has documented several more.

It was definitely substantiated in the Koulis case that the mystery liquid was not composed of human tears. A very different case cropped up seven years earlier in Italy in August, 1953, when a plaster statuette of the Immaculate Heart of Mary began to shed tears in the home of distraught and mentally disturbed Antonietta Janusso, a hysterical pregnant twenty-year-old girl prone to attacks of mutism, blindness, and convulsions. If nothing else, the Janusso Madonna was persistent. It continued to shed tears while placed on its side, while in the hands of a police inspector, and even when hanging outside the house! Chemical examination of the droplets revealed that they were indeed human tears.

According to Cassoli, there was a siege of weeping pictures after the Janusso case was made public. Blood dropped from a postcard portrait of the Madonna in Calagre, Italy; a newspaper cutout of the Virgin allegedly dripped water in Mezzolambardo; it was even reported that porcelain and papier-mâché figures throughout Italy were crying real tears. On the basis of their studies, both Fodor and Cassoli felt that to call these incidents "miracles" was a bit premature. They believed that the phenomena were caused psychically by the believers themselves.

It is tempting to compare Antonietta Janusso to the typical focus of a poltergeist attack. During poltergeist cases, the victimized family generally includes a disturbed person, usually but not always a child, around whom the phenomena center and who actually causes the destruction by unconsciously projecting mind over matter. Probably a similar syndrome causes the weeping Madonnas. Here, intense religious beliefs or conflicts erupt into open displays of psychic phenomena. But instead of the poltergeist's awesome and destructive displays, the phenomena take on purely religious overtones, as statues and pictures begin to weep or bleed. Sometimes these weeping figures herald more overt poltergeist action, but in the majority of cases the outbreak begins and ends with just the one incident.*

Even Fodor saw the connection. In comparing reports of bleeding and weeping objects to the usual poltergeist case he wrote:

> It follows that from a study of poltergeist cases in which the pubertal victim has intense religious feelings we may learn a good deal more about the weeping and bleeding religious statues than from religious ecstasies ...

Tears and water are not the only liquids that pictures and statues exude paranormally. As the above reports indicate, blood often precipitates as well. Not just red-colored liquid, but human blood! In the December, 1962, issue of *Esquire* magazine, the editors reproduced a photograph of a bleeding statue from the Hotel DuVar in Entrevaux, France, taken in 1954. The figure represented Saint Anne and belonged to M. Jean Salate, the owner of the hotel. Salate had purposely broken the hand of the statuette in a fit of anger and its finger dripped thirty drops of blood during the day and again the next morning. Chemical analysis proved that the liquid really was human blood. This case was predated by an almost identical case in 1949 in the United States. Little Shirley Anne Martin of Syracuse, New York, owned a small statue of St. Anne which wept after it had been broken.

A weeping cross has mystified investigators in Johannesburg, South Africa, according to a dispatch from Reuters. The cross was modeled and constructed after the First World War. On July 13, 1916, a ferocious battle raged in Delville Wood in France. By the time the bloody fighting was over, 2,000 South African soldiers had been killed. As a memorial to these soldiers, a cross was made from trees in the wood and sent to South Africa where it stands in a memorial

---

* A rather violent poltergeist outbreak occurred in Ireland in 1920. Pools of water appeared in the house, objects moved by themselves, and all the religious statues and pictures in the house dripped blood! (See Charles Fort's *Lo!* New York: Ace, n.d., pp. 46-47).

garden in Pietermaritzburg, Natal Province. Every July since the cross was made, it "weeps" on the anniversary of the battle. Resin flows from the two ends of the cross representing the points of crucifixion. Every year the cross is cleaned, yet, sure enough, on the next anniversary it again exudes resin.

One scientist who has examined the Delville Wood Cross is Henry Haigh, a research officer for South Africa's department of forestry. Haigh could come up with no normal explanation for the flows; he could only suggest that even after fifty years the wood had still not finished exuding its resin. Of course this doesn't explain why the phenomenon should correspond to the anniversary of the battle in which so many South African soldiers were slaughtered. Even Haigh had to admit that "It is very rare, even for slow-grown resinous wood to seep for more than two years."

A somewhat different "miracle" seriously disrupted the Bartolo family of Mexico City in 1961. Several years earlier, pretty seventeen-year-old Carmita had painted an image of the Virgin of Guadalupe. It took her only one long night to complete the painting. Three months later, she realized that in her haste to complete the portrait she had forgotten to sign it. She brought the painting up to her small studio, grabbed her brushes, and was about to autograph it when her elbow brushed against the canvas. It was warm! Puzzled, Carmita passed her hands over the painting and discovered that it was only that portion of the canvas around the Virgin's heart that was unnaturally warm.*

"Papa! Mama! Come here before I go crazy," shouted Carmita.

Both Mr. and Mrs. Bartolo examined the painting and found it warm. However, Bartolo was hardly a religious man and his advice was quick and to the point. "Put the Virgin inside your wardrobe and forget it," he urged. So the Bartolo Virgin became a family secret.

According to the testimony, locking away the painting only heralded one misfortune after another. Bartolo was a merchant, and during the next few months every conceivable misadventure struck his business, from ruined cargo shipments to bookkeeping errors. By this time even the gruff old

* The burning of the heart is also described by many saints and mystics. There are even cases where their hearts continued to emit heat after their deaths.

Mysteries and Miracles 41

wholesaler's skepticism about the picture was beginning to waver. So the family decided to consult Church authorities. Monsignor Aquilar investigated the painting, and even though he was impressed by the Virgin's warmth, his advice, ironically, was the same as Bartolo's—keep the painting a secret.

However, on July 16, 1961, the story leaked out after some guests of the Bartolos learned of the portrait. The tale soon spread throughout the town, and, as usual, throngs of the credulous and skeptical alike invaded the Bartolos' home. Since the public disclosure, Church authorities have kept a safe distance from the controversy. They have merely advised the family to keep the portrait within their home and have said that the Church would require a long time to investigate the enigma. Bartolo himself built an altar for the painting, and many visitors have claimed miraculous cures after praying before it. The only normal explanation for the heat that examiners could come up with was that perhaps the paint used for the portrait was acting like a photoelectric cell to generate heat, but that is pretty far-fetched. Perhaps Dr. Victor Sorial Jaimes, a physician who investigated the painting and who first suggested the photoelectric cell theory, summed up the situation best when he said, "I don't know what to think. Do you?"

I must admit that investigating such an incident is more difficult than checking into a bleeding or weeping Madonna. In the latter cases, one can gather up *physical* evidence of the phenomenon. Judging warmth by mere touch is more delicate. Apparently no one thought to hold a thermistor to the Bartolo painting to prove that it really was emitting heat. Or if someone did, no mention was made of it in the reports. Suggestion and belief are often factors that complicate cases such as these, as is evident in the following case.

Raymond Bayless and I were called in to investigate a heat-producing painting in 1973. The portrait, which was owned by a family in Los Angeles, was not a religious one. The owners claimed that the face would change expression (!) and that the back of it would become unnaturally warm. The picture had prompted serious inquiry: investigators from the University of California, Los Angeles, had taken an interest in the case, and Barry Taff, a young volunteer at the UCLA Neuropsychiatric Institute, had undertaken a lengthy investigation. He too felt that there was something peculiar about the painting including the warmth that radiated from it. Finally, an interview with the owners, along with the testimony of several investigators, was run as a feature story in Los Angeles-based *Probe* magazine.

Shortly after the publicity broke, Raymond and I learned that the painting had been lent by UCLA to Bart Ellis, a psychiatric social worker who was on the board of directors of the Southern California Society for Psychical Research. Bart called us and invited us to spend an evening with him and the picture at his West Los Angeles apartment. Despite the fact that many people had claimed that the painting became warm at night (not to mention changing its expression), neither Raymond, Bart, nor I felt any change in surface temperature. Our diagnosis? It was all probably sheer suggestion. People felt the warmth because they *expected* to feel it. Suggestion can cause all sorts of bizarre reactions, and mass suggestion can work just as well. (Remember Orson Welles' "War of the Worlds" panic of 1938?) Obviously the UCLA investigations weren't going too well either, for shortly after we babysat the portrait, the whole story drifted out of sight, sound ... and touch.

The above example illustrates the fact that stories of the miraculous cannot rest merely on human testimony. It often takes a little hand-soiling, on-the-spot investigation to validate and expose a weeping picture or bleeding statue. I say "expose," for it is a moot point just how many of these cases are the product not only of malobservation but of out-and-out fraud. Obviously many cases are undoubtedly genuine. The Janusso "miracle" is a case in point. But even the Church is often reluctant to involve itself in the investigation of a miracle, since fraud is so often at the root.

Probably the most thorough investigation of a bleeding statue was conducted at Mirebeau in Poitou, France, by Everard Feilding, an investigator for the Society for Psychical Research. The protagonist in the case was the Abbé Vachère, who was to undergo several heart-rending ordeals with both investigators and Church officials before the probe was concluded.

The case is an old one but unique in that more than one figure bled. According to reports which spread periodically through Europe between 1911 and 1913, Vachère was the center of a *series* of unexplainable manifestations. Two oleographs of the Sacred Heart bled, Hosts consecrated at Mass became covered with blood, and a statue of Christ also bled. A statue of the Virgin, placed in the same grotto as the Christ, wept as well.

The two pictures of the Sacred Heart had been given to the Abbé in 1906, but it wasn't until December, 1911, that the first bleeding occurred. The Abbé had gone to say Mass at 6:30 A.M. as usual when he noticed dark red marks on the forehead of Christ's portrait represented in one of the pictures. Several hours later, the mark had solidified, but during the next days it began to drip copious amounts of blood. By the end of the week, wounds representing the "crown of thorns" also appeared, and blood flowed from the hands and heart. A month later, blood began to appear on the consecrated Hosts, and the Abbé claimed that he could hear voices of lamentation emerging from the portrait.

In accordance with church requirements, Abbé Vachère notified Monsigneur Humbrecht of Poitiers, who requested that the picture be brought to the superior at the Seminary of Poitiers for examination. It was kept there for two months and then returned to Vachère with firm instructions that the matter remain secret and that the picture not be shown to anyone. But the phenomena became more intense.

As Feilding reports, the bleeding—and other manifestations reported by the Abbé—resumed at irregular intervals. The Abbé told Feilding that on May 27, 1912, he had just consecrated a Host when he noticed that a rent had appeared on it. He placed it aside, in order to consecrate another Host. However, as he proceeded, blood began to flow from the first Host. These flows continued for several months. Feilding actually saw the Host a year later. As he described it in his report, pools of blood had formed around the Host—which had been placed on the Church altar—and blood had run over the altar to the floor.

The next year brought with it further instructions from the Church. The Abbé was ordered by decree of the Holy Office to submit the picture to the local bishop. No sooner had this order reached Vachère than another picture, a replica of the first which was housed in the Abbé's cottage, began to bleed and weep. Everard Feilding was hot on the trail of the case at the time of these developments and was able to investigate the picture himself.

In order to carry out his investigation, Feilding asked if he could see the picture himself. The Abbé agreed, but apologized, saying that the picture was not bleeding at the present time. Nevertheless, he fetched the key to the cottage, in which the picture hung, and let Feilding in. The investigator could see immediately that reddish serum was running from the eyes of the portrait, and took a sample of the liquid for future analysis. No new flows began as he and the Abbé watched, so they aborted their vigil and returned to the Chapel. There, the Abbé showed Feilding several other Hosts which were soaked in blood.

Unfortunately, Feilding could not have chosen a worse time for an investigation. France was filled with rumors of war, and with the European political and military scene so delicate, he had to take his leave and return to England. However, he took with him a sample of the serum removed from the picture, which he turned over to a bacteriologist at the Lister Institute for analysis. This examination proved that the liquid was definitely *not* human blood but was contaminated by a tiny organism usually found in stagnant water. This was a disappointment to Feilding since a previous chemical analysis of another sample of serum made in Germany by another investigator had shown it to be human blood. As Feilding pointed out, however, it really made little difference *what* the fluid was. Certainly, if the serum was human blood this would be in accordance with the theory that a miracle was taking place. But if the Vachère phenomenon was some type of purely psychic manifestation, the physical composition of the liquid would be of only secondary importance in determining and substantiating that the actual flow had no normal explanation. Of course, human blood would be harder to fake than colored liquid for obvious reasons. Feilding could not believe, at least at this point, that the Abbé was faking the phenomenon. If he were, surely he would have objected to having samples of the blood taken back to England for analysis—and ultimate exposure.

It wasn't until two years later that Feilding was able to pay a return visit to Abbé Vachère. The war was raging, and even the Abbé warned him not to come to France, but the investigator's curiosity got the better of him. He arrived in Poitou without warning. At that time he learned that the past two years had brought Vachère nothing but misfortune. Although no official inquiry had been carried out by the Church, he had been condemned by the Bishop and excommunicated by Rome. The civil authorities even suspected that the Abbé was sympathetic to the Germans.

Despite this awful state of affairs, the second picture still continued to bleed. On going to the chapel, Feilding found it soaked with red residue. For three days he stayed at the Mirebeau chapel, and every time he visited the picture, it was sopping with red moisture, no matter how carefully he had previously dried it. In true detective fashion, Feilding asked if he could lock and seal the chapel door to make sure no one had access to the picture. The request deeply offended the Abbé, but he allowed the door to be locked and let Feilding keep the key. While closing the chapel, Feilding secretly rigged the door with a piece of paper that would dislodge if someone tried to open it with a duplicate key. Hours later, Feilding once again found the picture wet, but the paper had been disturbed, which indicated that someone had tampered with the door. Feilding reported the facts to the Abbé, who burst into a rage, arguing that perhaps his sacristan had tried to gain entrace to the room not knowing that it was supposed to be kept locked. However, the fact remained that Feilding had still not been able to watch the painting *begin* to emit the liquid. He had watched it time and time again, but no blood would flow. It was only after he left the chapel and then returned that he found the picture drenched. Although he was becoming somewhat suspicious, he could not believe that the Abbé was faking the miracle. If he had, all it had achieved was his excommunication, the alienation of his parishioners, and the suspicion of the local authorities.

Since Feilding had to leave Mirebeau again, he arranged for a friend of his, Mme. J. Lichnerowicz, to visit the Abbé and continue the investigation. She was not to divulge to the Abbé that she had consulted with Feilding. Mme. Lichnerowicz visited the Abbé in 1916 and 1917 and reported back to Feilding in England. Luckily she was able to witness the bleeding from the beginning, and she watched the blood actively flowing, a goal Feilding had failed to achieve. She wrote enthusiatically:

> I saw a linen cloth become covered with blood before my eyes as follows. The Abbé had, while I watched him, placed a piece of white linen under the picture, and in front of me the blood continued to flow with sufficient speed to soak into the whole of the linen in the space of about an hour. It seems that such intense manifestations as these are rare...

When Feilding again visited the Abbé in 1920, it was on his honeymoon. The Abbé was still excommunicated but had rejected Rome's authority and, counter to papal decree, was continuing to celebrate Mass. A small statue of Christ was now the center of the bleeding, and it was at this point that the first definite suspicion of fraud arose. Upon hearing the story of the bleeding statue, Feilding went to examine it. All he could see were dried bloodstains. But as he was looking at the figure, his wife thought she saw the Abbé sprinkle some water on a picture. Soon after, he called Feilding's attention to the picture, and indeed it was dripping with red drops of liquid.

I do feel compelled to comment on this charge by Mrs. Feilding inasmuch as it was the only serious charge ever made against the Abbé. First, in looking over her deposition, it is clear that she only saw the Abbé wave his hand in the general direction of the painting. She did not actually see him throw any liquid at all. Secondly, Mrs. Feilding was formerly Stanislawa Tomczyk, a celebrated Polish physical medium who was given to making rather wild charges of fraud against "competitors" and who, on several occasions, disrupted séances to which she was invited, so her testimony must be taken with a grain of salt. She made it clear that she considered the whole subject of psychic phenomena suspect, which is rather odd since she herself was a medium of considerable note!

Nonetheless, Feilding was able to take with him more samples of the liquid, which he again submitted to the same bacteriologist. On this occasion, *the samples were identified as human blood*. A second opinion was sought and this independent test also certified that the fluid was human blood.

Feilding, who was himself Catholic, tried unsuccessfully to get Church officials to investigate the blood phenomenon but to no avail. The Church was suspicious and reluctant, and the Abbé was uncompromising and obstinate. By 1921, the Abbé was dead, and the case was over. But Feilding did discover that before the Abbé's death, pictures were known to bleed and weep in homes that he had merely visited. Feilding remained baffled by the case to the end of his life.

There is little doubt that there was a great mystery at the Abbé Vachère's church which has never been solved. It is hard to believe that he was a hoaxer, for his only rewards were the utter disdain of Church officials and his eventual excommunication. Those who knew him described him as almost childlike, devout, giving, but obstinate. Other than Mrs. Feilding's rather cryptic charge, there was no evidence that the Abbé was perpetrating a hoax. On the other hand, there is substantial evidence that the Abbé was *paranormally* responsible for the outbreaks. The fact that so many of the religious objects he owned, and even those in the homes he visited, bled would confirm that through some psychic force the Abbé was able to materialize blood onto objects close to him. Where the blood or liquid came from is a puzzle that will probably never be solved.

Bleeding and weeping Madonnas do not actually *emit* blood or tears. It is more likely that somehow liquid materializes around or on the objects. As indicated earlier, pools of liquid are often found during poltergeist outbreaks. Several examples could be cited. In a poltergeist case in Methuen, Massachusetts, in 1963, water popped out of walls, to the consternation of a local family. When they moved to a neighboring town to stay with relatives, water was ejected from the walls of that house as well! These water flows continued even when the water to the house was turned off. Earlier I cited a water poltergeist studied in Germany.

But what about blood? There is little doubt in my mind that in some of these cases human blood does precipitate on religious objects. In the Vachère and Hotel DuVar cases, the fact that the precipitation was actually real blood, not just colored liquid, seems proved. This leads us to another area of investigation, one of the rarest of all psychic manifestations: blood apports. In some cases, large amounts of human blood spontaneously appear in a house or church, in and out of a religious context. The phenomenon is so rare that I have been able to find only a handful of cases in psychic literature that even mention it. But these few cases do have a significant bearing on bleeding and weeping pictures and statues, for they show that the human mind is actually capable of materializing blood.

One eyewitness to a case of a blood apport was the Reverend Charles Tweedale, the minister of Weston Vicarage, who was also an active investigator of all things psychic. During his tenure as minister, he often confronted the paranormal and wrote several books on his experiences. He was also an amateur astronomer and a violin-maker of some note. In his *News from the Next World* he records from his diaries:

> May 1st, 1929—A very extraordinary happening befell me today at Church. I had a funeral, attended by a great concourse of people, of a man who had stabbed himself in the throat and died most miserably as the result of the act. The poor fellow had been ill for a long time, and the case excited much sympathy. The result was that a long procession of people accompanied his body to the churchyard. When I met the procession at the gate I asked the relatives what the verdict of the inquest was, and after some questioning was reluctantly told that it was one of *felo-de-se*. I then addressed them saying, "Good people, by the law of the Church I am not allowed to receive this body into the Church, nor am I allowed to say the service over it. Therefore it will have to be taken to the graveside and buried without service." At this, suppressed groans and murmurings passed along the procession, and I saw that the decision would be greatly resented and cause much pain to relatives and friends. I therefore resolved to risk it, and turning to the people I told them how I sympathized with them and as this seemed to be a case in which there were extenuating circumstances I would, on my own responsibility, allow them to bring the body into the Church. They did so, and we had a very impressive service which they followed with the closest attention. Proceeding to the grave I then "committed the body to the ground" and returned to Church. Going into the vestry I plunged my hand into my trouser pocket for the keys of the safe (which was smooth and polished) to get out the Registry of Burial, and opening the safe got out the volume, and sitting down before the table I filled up the Register with name, date, and full particulars, and then signed it with my name. I had just done this and *my hand was still on the paper* when I was amazed to see a *big drop of blood* well up *quickly* from the back of my hand on the clear white smooth skin where there was no scratch. It rose up swiftly and became so big that it began to roll down, and I had to tilt the hand sideways to prevent it falling on to the book alongside of my signature. (I have often regretted that I did not allow it to do so.) Scarcely able to credit the evidence of my senses I ran out of Church with my hand clenched and extended and told the three men who were filling up the grave, at the same time showing them the blood-drop on the back of my hand. They had examined it with the greatest astonishment and were profoundly impressed. After the blood was wiped from my hand, *no more blood appeared*—the

manifestation consisted of just one big drop, welling up until it was the bigness of a pea. This was the first and only case of the burial of a suicide that I have had in this parish, and the first case I ever had of a person who cut himself, and that the blood-drop should thus rise up on the back of my hand at the critical moment of signing my name to his burial is beyond all chance or coincidence ...

An even more bizarre rash of blood apportations occurred in the home of Helen Lambert during her many psychic experiments with the St. Louis medium Will Hannegan. On one occasion her maid had just left the bedroom after cleaning the furniture and as Mrs. Lambert was dressing for dinner. When she had finished, she left to attend to her dinner guests but then excused herself in order to return to her room. There she found a stream of thick blood running down the length of a cabinet, forming a pool at its base. Mrs. Lambert quickly summoned another maid, thinking perhaps that the maid who had cleaned the furniture had cut herself. The ensuing commotion brought the news of the blood materialization to the guests, who rushed into the room to see the mysterious manifestation. By this time, the maid had brought in a towel to clean up the mess. Everyone was still discussing the incident when the maid's voice jolted them:

"What kind of blood is this? It has all gone from the towel," she exclaimed in bewilderment. All the guests inspected the towel and indeed the blood had vanished as mysteriously as it had appeared. The whole incident, brief though it was, was over.

Even the great French parapsychologist Dr. Gustave Geley once saw a drop of blood suddenly materialize on a photograph of a murdered man.

These cases alert us to an important fact—that bleeding religious objects are in themselves not miraculous. They are not caused by the will of God superseding physical laws. Instead we can better understand them as psychic effects.

There is no doubt in my mind that the psychic abilities of the witnesses are causing this type of materialization. No doubt it was Reverend Lewis himself who brought about the water that appeared on his grandmother's photograph. Similarly, the Abbé's simple and almost superstitious religious devotion was the psychic seed from which flowed the blood on the pictures and statues in his church and abode. Tweedale's religious conflicts over admitting a suicide for Christian burial probably caused the sign of blood on his hand as he completed the record of the service. Note how in each case the "miracle" seems directly related to some deep-seated conflict. What of the weeping cross in South Africa? This effect calls for an even more complicated explanation. Perhaps the group emotion of the soldiers and survivors of the battle was so intense that it projected a lasting psychic influence on the wood from which the cross was fashioned. This lingering psychic force might regulate and cause the seepage of sap inherent in the wood for years to come. In this respect the object is acting like a miniature haunted house. A haunting is set up when a tragedy and the strong emotions accompanying it contaminate a house, church, or other structure. These emotions somehow are ingrained into the structure and periodically cause the scenes of the disaster to replay themselves. Apparitions are seen, footsteps are heard, and phantom dramas are reenacted. It is as though a motion picture of the events had been projected onto the atmosphere. Sometimes these residues even have physical side effects. I once stayed in a haunted house during which time the bed in which I slept was shaken every night for about a week. The weeping cross of South Africa might be similarly affected by some sort of psychic field which reactivates the seepage on every anniversary of the Delville Wood tragedy.

Additional evidence that what we call miracles are actually collective psychic projections can be witnessed by anyone willing to travel to Naples to see "the Miracle of St. Januarius" which has been celebrated for centuries and for which no scientific explanation has ever been found. Yet several times a year the miracle is repeated at Naples Cathedral to the consternation of scientists, the Church (which has never offically declared it a miracle), and to believers and skeptics alike.

The source of the miracle dates back 1,600 years to the day of St. Januarius' beheading. After the execution, his blood was collected by his followers and a vial of this now-dried blood is still held in veneration in Naples. Several times a year, Mass is said over the vial and the blood liquefies. Although thousands of people have seen the miracle, no normal explanation has yet been found for it.

In 1970, Giorgio Giorgi, an Italian physician, traveled to the Cathedral to see the miracle firsthand and to determine if

Mysteries and Miracles

he could detect any normal cause for it. Giorgi was within five feet of the vial as the Archbishop began the ceremony by invoking the saint while slowly rotating the vial for all to see. During this initial period the contents of the vial were clearly solid. The rotation had lasted for only about four minutes when, as Giorgi reported:

> I saw, and this was a most disconcerting fact, just in front of my nose at a distance of a little over three feet, that the clot of blood had suddenly changed from the solid state into that of a liquid. The changing over from the solid to a liquid state happened all of a sudden, unexpectedly. The liquid itself had become much brighter, more shining; inside the liquid many gaseous bubbles appeared, so much so that the liquid (shall we call it blood?) seemed to be in a state of ebullition. While at first, still in the solid state, the clot filled about one-third of the phial, after its liquification the substance occupied seven-tenths of the phial.

Giorgi was able to handle the vial himself immediately following the "miracle." The bottle was cool, indicating that no heat had been applied to it. It should be added that spectroscopic analysis of the material has substantiated that it actually is blood. Fraud seems very unlikely. The miracle was first reported in the fourteenth century, and it is hard to believe that it could have been perpetrated by so many different clergymen over a period of 500 years! No chemical or purely physical explanation for the liquefaction can be found either.

The Miracle of St. Januarius is especially convincing inasmuch as the phenomenon has been publicly witnessed over 10,000 times before millions of onlookers. Still, though, I think it is possible to find a psychic, not divine, explanation for the event. On the one hand the blood might have been affected psychically at the time of Januarius' death. The process of psychic liquefaction might be similar to the effect that causes the Pietermaritzburg Cross to weep. In other words, some psychic field is affecting the blood which regulates when it liquefies and when it hardens. On the other hand, another likely explanation could be that the act of veneration and celebration by the crowds of the devout projects a collective psychic force that acts on the vial. This is not as farfetched as it might sound. Parapsychology has learned that many people can project minute amounts of PK energy. J. B. Rhine and his co-workers, who started studying psychokinesis at Duke University in the 1930s, discovered that many everyday nonpsychic people could psychically deflect drops of water or influence the fall of dice. During the celebration of St. Januarius, could the setting, the close identification of the religious to him and to each other, and their own belief work so that a collective PK force is projected from them which acts on the vial? This is a theory worth considering. Certainly it is no more bizarre than believing in a divine miracle.

Another series of phenomena that seem linked to some sort of collective psychic influence which can affect a material object are those instances in which faces appear on walls. These extremely unusual cases have often been heralded as miraculous by the religious. There are several on record in which portraits of Christ, Mary, or deceased Church prelates have mysteriously appeared on the walls of churches or rectories. However, wall faces are also known to appear in nonreligious settings as well. Although these occurrences are extremely rare, they came to the attention of psychic investigators recently due to one case in Belméz, Spain, and another in a little town in New Mexico.

On June 7, 1975, the *Topeka State Journal* ran a short story about a rather bizarre apparition that appeared on the wall of a small church in Holman, New Mexico. The story reported that "scores of persons are flocking nightly to a small chapel in this north New Mexico village in hopes of catching a glimpse of Jesus Christ. The Reverend Leonard Bayer, priest at St. Gertrude Parish in nearby Mora, said an apparition of Jesus has appeared nightly for the past two weeks on a wall at the Immaculate Heart of Mary Church." Father Bayer told reporters that the apparition resembled "a charcoal drawing" and added that the figure portrayed Jesus "with a beard and long hair, just as our Lord appeared in some pictures we have of Him." The apparition appeared at night and was not always visible when viewed at short-range. It would become more clearly defined when seen from a distance.

The apparitional face first appeared on May 18th. Two teen-age boys were the first to discover the image. Frightened, they ran to report the phantom to neighbors. Among the apparition-watchers since then have been Reverend Lucien Hendron, chancellor of the archdiocese of Santa Fe, and Mora County Sheriff Palimon Chavez who told a *National Enquirer* reporter, "I was pretty skeptical until I saw it myself."

The image itself was about four feet by two feet and appeared on the wall some seven feet from the ground. The figure seemed to emerge from the spotted configuration of the concrete and did not resemble a drawing or photo projection.

Of course, the devout who came to see the apparition were firm in their conviction that a miracle had been bestowed upon them. Visitors flocked to Holman in such droves to see the "miracle" that traffic became a problem. "Why, just the other night we had 4,000 cars in Holman," reported Sheriff Chavez to on-the-spot reporters. Since the phantom face has gained publicity it has been photographed and shown on nationwide news telecasts.

The Holman case is very similar to another psychic portrait of Christ which appeared on a freshly painted wall in the Tabernacle of Glad Tidings, in Nassau, Bahamas, on January 20, 1963. During the regular Sunday sermon, one of the parishioners, Mrs. Euna Laine, cried out, "I see Jesus! I see Jesus! I see Christ! He is here!" At first, not everyone could see the dim outline of the portrait. Resembling a charooal sketch, it seemed to be formed out of configurations on the wall and gradually became more definite during the next several days. Luther Evans, a reporter from the Chicago *Daily News*, traveled to the Bahamas to see the odd configuration. By then, *three* distinct faces had emerged from the wall. As Evan approached the wall, the faces became less obvious, but like the Holman figure they were best seen, as is a fine painting, from a distance of several feet.

Despite the publicity over these apparitions, they are not novel in the history of psychic studies. Many such faces have emerged from the walls of churches. In fact, there is quite a history behind this phenomenon.

Perhaps the most famous case concerns Dean John Liddell, who died in 1898. Years later, in 1923, reports were rife that a picture of the famous Oxford cleric had miraculously appeared on a plaster wall in Christ Church Cathedral. The face was alleged to have emerged right out of the wall near a tablet erected to his memory. These reports were soon verified, as hundreds of spectators flocked to see the detailed portrait. In his *Between Two Worlds*, psychic investigator Nandor Fodor reported that the Liddell face, "appeared as if the mineral salts of the plaster were slowly undergoing the same type of chemical change as the salts of silver on a photographic plate." Years later, another face appeared, that of a woman which was said to bear a resemblance to Mrs. Liddell. The Liddell case caused considerable publicity. *Cassell's Weekly* reported on the face in 1926, commenting on its clarity and how it did not seem etched but rather masterfully constructed within the wall. The faces were still visible in 1931.

Church authorities are notoriously antagonistic to anything suggesting the supernatural. Even considering the rich psychic heritage of the saints and mystics, the Church, Catholic or Anglican, is very wary of the miraculous. It seeks to cover it up, expose it, or at least discourage people from paying much attention to it. The case of the phantom face of Dean Liddell is typical. Sometime in either 1931 or 1932, Church officials erected a new altar in Christ Church directly in front of the psychic portraits, concealing them forever.

Actually, Dean Liddell inspired more psychic events than merely the faces. The following story comes to us from Reverend Charles Tweedale as he reported it in *News from the Next World*. He had just heard about the masking of the Liddell faces when his daughter saw an apparition of the clergyman in the Tweedale home. Through Mrs. Tweedale's automatic writing, Dean Liddell communicated to complain of the concealment. This could have been due purely to suggestion, since Mrs. Tweedale already knew of the recent attempt to hide the faces. But although she had never seen a picture of the Dean, she was able to draw a remarkable likeness of him through her psychic talents. Tweedale wrote to the new Dean of Christ Church, Dean Williams, asking why the new altar had been erected and why the faces had been plastered over and defaced. Williams replied that while nothing had been done to ruin the configurations, it had been decided by Church officials to hide them with the new altar.

Attempting to discover why the face should have appeared after so many years Nandor Fodor tried to trace the history behind the Liddell face, and he came up with what he thought was the answer. The face, he claimed, began to form on the very day that a reconciliation had been effected between two feuding branches of the Dean's own family—the Liddells and the Ravenworths. In fact, a celebration had been held that very day to mark the occasion.

Another phantom face had appeared previously in an English church in 1897, two weeks after the death of Charles John Vaughan, Dean of Llandaff. The face appeared on the west wall of Llandaff Cathedral and was remarkably lifelike. Church authorities attributed it to a freak configuration caused by damp spots.

Luckily, the Vaughan face, when photographed, showed the clear initials D.V. as part of the portrait. Mr. W. Sharp, the photographer, traced the history of the portrait and wrote to Fodor, "Dean Vaughan was attached to Llandaff Cathedral for a great number of years. Shortly after his death ... damp stain started to appear on the left-hand side of the main entrance to Llandaff Cathedral. The stain just seemed to grow until at last it had produced a striking likeness of the late Dean, even the letters D.V. forming on the side of the face."

The ultimate fate of the psychic portrait fared little better than that of Liddell's. Cathedral officials placed a notice board over the "damp spot," which had begun to fade, and ordered that it not to be removed.

Churches are not the only places that house phantom faces. One correspondent wrote to Fodor to tell how the figure of his deceased wife gradually formed on his bathroom wall! But the most bizarre of all these wall faces are those that continuously appear in a "haunted" house in Belméz, Spain. The case has been investigated by the well-known German parapsychologist, Dr. Hans Bender, of the University of Freiburg. The faces began to emerge right out of the concrete on the walls and floor of a small, modest house in the fall of 1971. They were crude, not very artistic, almost caricatures. The first ones to appear so frightened the family that they were destroyed, but soon the house became a local tourist attraction, which caused considerable consternation among the local authorities.

Spain has very little psychic research, and anything miraculous causes utmost concern to the local government and the Church. In this instance, the town officials closed the house to visitors, and a Catholic priest started a rumor that the whole thing was a fraud. This rumor—for it was nothing more—was soon exploded.

However, Belméz officials did allow Dr. Bender to investigate since, as one of Europe's best-known researchers, he was eminently qualified. Bender was not able to actually witness the appearance of the faces during his probe, but several faces were still on the walls; they appeared to have been formed right out of configurations in the concrete. Once formed, the faces were stable and remained permanently on the walls and floors. The kitchen was the main center for these appearances.

Bender did conduct one experiment in order to rule out the normal suspicion that someone was darting about drawing the faces. His team of researchers placed a sheet of light, transparent plastic over the floor, hoping that the faces would appear under it. Although nothing appeared during his stay, the faces did continue to form after he left and while the sheet was still in place. Bender wrote to me about this experiment: "I attached a plastic plate on the cement floor where the faces appear, as a safeguard from fraud. This plate had to be taken off last month, as condensed water under the plate made continous observation impossible. Faces are said to have appeared under the plate, but the photographer spoilt the photos."

The plastic cover was removed in front of official witnesses. The kitchen was then locked so that no one could disturb the room while the floor dried out. When the floor was clear, new faces were found. When a new kitchen was built onto the house, the faces appeared there as well, and they continued to form up until 1973.

So the Holman, New Mexico, apparitional portrait was not the first of its kind, nor will it be the last. When we think about psychic phenomena, we all too often think only about ESP, mind over matter, etc. Wall faces are only one manifestation of a whole world of psychic mysteries that lie beyond ESP and psychokinesis. Hopefully, as parapsychology leaves the lab, it may turn its attention to these enigmas.

A possible explanation for these cases is that group emotion caused the appearance of the faces. In the cases of the deceased prelates, it could be that the phenomenon represents an act of veneration by the congregation. In the Belméz case, it is likely that some psychic atmosphere pervaded the house in the form of a haunting that manifested itself by causing faces to appear.

Another group of phenomena that demonstrates the existence of a collective psychic force projected by the living is what I call "imitative miracles." A miracle or religious event occurs in one church, and as publicity about it spreads, parallel cases start to crop up all over the country. In these cases, it looks as if some collective mind in the congregation seeks to imitate a miracle that first occurred elsewhere. Perhaps it can be called psychic one-upmanship.

For example, an epidemic of glowing crosses appearing on

church windows spread over the United States in 1971. It all started on August 27, 1971, at Faith Baptist Church in Los Angeles. The first appearance of the glowing cross was not a very auspicious event. It happened after a rather ill-fated choir rehearsal. The rehearsal had gone poorly because the head of the choir, Mrs. Mabel Davis, had not even been able to find a suitable organist as an accompanist. With thoughts of resigning filling her head, she was about to leave the church when her eleven-year-old daughter cried out and pointed to the window. There, in full radiance at the back of the church, was what Mrs. Davis described as "a great gleaming golden cross shining in the window."

After news stories appeared in the local press, hundreds of visitors flocked to the church to see the cross of light which usually appeared only after 4:00 P.M. as the sun began to shine through the back window. Of course, this immediately caused investigators to dismiss the cross as a freak product of light refraction. But why did the cross appear all of a sudden? The window had been there for years, and no cross had previously appeared on it.

Even if the Faith Baptist Church cross was caused by normal refraction, the event sparked a series of parallel miracles across the country. Only two weeks later, a cross illuminated the window of the First Born Holiness Church, in Apalachicola, Florida. It appeared for several days and was seen by thousands of parishioners and townfolk. The mayor asked the physics department of Florida State University to investigate, but there is no public record of any official report. However, Dr. K. P. Chapman, a science photographer, examined the window and concluded that "there is no doubt that the cross observed is an optical effect produced by the light and the particular type of window glass." But again we are faced with that gnawing question: Why did it take so long for this refraction to occur? And why only two weeks after the Los Angeles case?

The first appearance of the Florida cross was on September 12th. On September 22nd, and then a week later, fiery crosses were reported from two more churches in Florida, one at United Methodist Church in Mexico City and the other at St. John's Baptist Church in Panama City. Three more cases erupted in Florida within the next month. Perhaps the most sensational of these was the one at Paxton Revival Center in Jacksonville. The cross was first seen shining through a window by two young parishioners. Reverend

James W. Dobbs was at first rather dubious about the authenticity of the cross, but gradually accepted it as a miracle. His church was flooded with photographers and newsmen, and during an interview for the *Florida Times Union*, Reverend Dobbs made an almost unbelievable statement. "They took Polaroid pictures," he said, "and when they were developed you could see Jesus' hands on some of the pictures. And some showed spikes through the hands."

Had I not seen one of these photographs myself I would have dismissed this report. But when I did see it, my skepticism shriveled. One picture, which was subsequently published in the June, 1972, issue of *Fate* magazine accompanying an article, "A Flap of Glowing Crosses" by associate editor David Techter, clearly shows this effect. On the left-hand side of the crossbeam is a clear representation of a hand, four fingers outstretched with a fifth (the thumb?) crossing over them. The right side of the cross is less distinct but shows a large, black, nail-like protuberance at the spot where the crucified hand of Christ would normally lie. If anything, the Paxton Revival Center cross was no normal light refraction!

Soon the phenomenon, which had started in Los Angeles before spreading to Florida, began to break through both geographical and denominational lines. Cases cropped up in Seventh-Day Adventist, Methodist, and Church of God houses of worship. By the end of October, crosses had appeared in the windows of some seven churches in Georgia alone.

Perhaps the most interesting case in this epidemic appeared not in an elaborate church or cathedral but in New York, in the heart of the Bronx slums. The case is unique because it was one of the first to occur in a secular setting. The cross began to materialize on a window at Number 1, 835 Trinity Avenue. Interestingly enough, the dazzling cross appeared only after the primary witness, Mrs. Viola Mitchell, had read an account of the Georgia cases.

Of course, there were many attempts to explain away the sightings. The Brunswick Glass Company, a manufacturer of glass used for church windows, put the rash of cases down to a flaw in the structure of the glass. They had produced the glass used for many of the churches involved in Georgia and willingly took the blame (or credit?) for the incidents.

But the Brunswick confession leaves even more questions unanswered. The crosses were seen in Florida, New York, and California; the "refractions" spread as if an intelligence were behind the incidents. Moreover, the glass windows had been installed for years and no refraction had ever occurred before. No doubt some or even many of the reports *were* due to normal causes, but many of them defy a purely physical explanation.

The cross flap of 1971 is one of those oddities that will never be explained. It is my guess that the cause was psychic. Perhaps the original Los Angeles cross was caused by refraction, but whatever the case, when congregations all over the country heard about it they too, even if on a subconscious level, became absorbed in the phenomenon. Gradually they exerted a group psychic influence onto windows in their own churches. This could have (1) caused the cross, or (2) deflected normal sunlight coming into the churches in order to refract it in just such a way as to produce the appearance of a cross. Once this "psychic sphere of influence" was set up, it might decay only gradually. Thus the crosses could continue to appear for several days. I think a similar sphere of influence can account for bleeding and weeping statues, icons, paintings, and crosses as well. It shouldn't be hard to test this theory experimentally. Perhaps in the future some physicist will project light through a prism or glass panel and see if the light waves can be influenced by a psychic's or a group's PK.

That man can exert a psychic influence on normal phenomena of nature (such as light refraction) is also given some support when we consider an even odder phenomenon which was mentioned by Charles Fort in his last book, *Wild Talents*. Fort called the enigma "a shower of virgins." This was a fall of hailstones with the portrait of the Virgin Mary imprinted on some of them! The incident occurred in Remiremont, France, on May 26, 1907.

As might be expected, the "miracle" did not seem unrelated to some religiously based frustrations in the community itself. Only a few days before, the town council raised the ire of the townspeople by forbidding a religious procession and during the next few days, the town's sense of anger, fervor, and religious devotion grew and grew. And then the hailstones came.

The Abbé Gueniot, one of the chief witnesses to the events, reported how he first became aware of the uncanny nature of the storm when a member of his household ran in, announcing that extraordinary hailstones were plunging to the earth, carrying an image of the Blessed Virgin.

"In order to satisfy her," reported the Abbé, "I glanced

carelessly at the hailstones, which she held in her hand. But since I did not want to see anything, and moreover could not do so without my spectacles, I turned to go back to my book. She urged: 'I beg of you to put on your glasses.' I did so, and saw very distinctly on the front of the hailstones, which were slightly convex in the center, although the edges were somewhat worn, the bust of a woman, with a robe that was turned up at the bottom, like a priest's cope. I should, perhaps, describe it more exactly by saying that it was like the Virgin of the Hermits. The outline of the images was slightly hollow, as if they had been formed with a punch, but were very boldly drawn. Mlle. André asked me to notice certain details of the costume, but I refused to look at it any longer. I was ashamed of my credulity, feeling sure that the Blessed Virgin would hardly concern herself with instantaneous photographs on hailstones. I said, 'But do not you see that these hailstones have fallen on vegetables, and received these impressions? Take them away: they are no good to me.' I returned to my book, without giving further thought to what had happened. But my mind was disturbed by the singular formation of these hailstones. I picked up three in order to weigh them, without looking closely. They weighed between six and seven ounces. One of them was perefctly round, like balls with which children play, and had a seam all around it, as though it had been cast in a mold."

When the Abbé reexamined the stones and saw the obvious female figure imprinted upon them, he changed his opinion and came to the conclusion that nothing but a divine explanation could account for the incident.

But there were even more mysteries connected with the hailstones. As anyone knows who has ever been caught in the Midwest during a hailstorm, these balls can cause serious damage. They can destroy whole fields of crops and even damage buildings. At Remiremont, witnesses testified that the normal, unmarked hailstones had in fact been responsible for much damage, but the miraculous hailstones had not. They appeared as though falling lightly from only a few yards in the air and caused no harm when they landed. Over fifty witnesses supported the various statements made about the miracle.

The facts about the subsidence of the hailstones demonstrate that there was a psychic influence on the stones. The odd behavior is very typical of poltergeist outbreaks, where objects and rocks are hurled about but do little personal harm if and when they strike people. I think we can find a similar

Mysteries and Miracles

explanation for the Remiremont hailstones very much like the one we suggested as the cause of the 1971 mystery crosses. The townsfolk were in a heated fervor which projected a collective psychic force able fo interact with the natural forces that formed the hailstones. The psychic influence guided the formation of some of the stones, so that they were created with impressions of the Virgin.

A similar process can also explain what occurs at religious revivals and other mass gatherings during which spectacular visual psychic demonstrations are often a by-product. These cases will be the last group of miracles that I will discuss.

Probably no revival in history can compare with the incredible mania that spread over South Wales in 1904 and 1905. Although South Wales had been the scene of growing religious sentiment during earlier years, it was not until the appearance of a fiery young preacher named Evan Roberts that the revival broke in full force. Spurred on by his private religious and visionary experiences, Roberts, who had originally trained as a Calvinist Methodist preacher, mounted a crusade throughout Wales where his powerful oratory and extraordinary charisma soon catapulted the area into a religious frenzy. At first, people flocked to hear him speak; then spontaneous revivals broke out in hamlets all through the country. The news media was soon on the trail, and all the Welsh papers were carrying the story of Roberts' revival. While he was not the direct cause of the revival, his uncanny powers caused a public zeal within the Welsh people that only died down a year later. First one village would be the scene of almost frantic public religious demonstrations, then, like an infection, the revival would spread to neighboring hamlets. Then psychic phenomena began: mysterious music would be heard in the air, great crosses and shafts of lights would appear in the sky, people were transfigured or spoke in tongues, and great orbs of light would stream forth from the heavens. Hundreds of people were witness to these displays.

Aerial lights were perhaps the most commonly witnessed phenomena during these revivals. The lights took various shapes from will-'o-the-wispish orbs hovering or darting just over the ground to huge discs in the sky. There were hundreds of sightings during this period. As Fryer tells us, one witness testified:

"I have seen [the light] every night from the beginning of the Revival about six weeks ago. Sometimes it appears like a motorcar lamp flashing and going out and injuring nothing at all; other times like two lamps and tongues of fire all round them, going out in one place and lighting again in another place far off sometimes, other times a quick flash and going out immediately, and when the fire goes out a vapor of smoke comes in its place, also a rainbow of vapor and a very bright star."

Another witness described the light as, "... hovering above a certain farmhouse and it appeared to me as three lamps almost three yards apart ... very brilliant and dazzling, moving and jumping like a sea-wave under the influence of the sun on a very hot day. The light continued so for ten minutes."

These lights were seen from 1904 to 1905. Sometimes several lights would appear, or groups of tiny lights would form, surrounding a larger one; sometimes they would form pillars or move about or flash on and off. Even geographical areas not contaminated by the South Wales religious frenzy were invaded by these aerial acrobatics. Pillars of fire in the sky were reported in North Wales in January, 1905, and were witnessed by townspeople who had not been influenced by the revival in the south. During the appearance of these lights, physical objects close to them became illuminated by a soft glow. This is a feature which we will note again—in Egypt in 1968!

Just when and where the lights appeared seemed pretty random, but on occasion they would appear at the height of a religious service or revival meeting. For example, the revival had spread to the hamlet of Ynysybwl where the Reverend Jones, another revival leader, began a month of preaching in July, 1905. It wasn't until three weeks later, though, that the glowing discs made their appearance. Jones was now speaking in a neighboring town, and several citizens went to hear him. On their return to Ynysybwl they organized their own revival meeting in the town square, complete with preaching, confessions, and singing whch had lasted for several hours when a shining light, which one witness described as a "ball of light about the size of the moon," appeared directly above them. As they watched in amazement, little darts of light shot from the orb as it ascended into the heavens, growing brighter but smaller at the same time. Another witness, who was not at the revival, saw a zigzagging light over the hill-studded horizon several days later. Sometimes the lights would be seen traversing the skies, stopping at various points on the horizon, usually hovering above areas where revival meetings were in progress.

However, the most spectacular light displays did not seem to relate to the mass revival demonstration but instead appeared to follow one individual, Mrs. Mary Jones, a woman preacher who had received, she claimed, a direct call from God to preach. Her powerful oratory, the exciting accounts of her personal and often ecstatic visions, and her unbelievable fervor as she preached soon catapulted her into a position rivaling Evan Roberts as the prime figure in the revival. Wherever she preached, the aerial lights seemed to follow. A reporter from the *Daily Mail* traveled to the town where Mary Jones had just spoken in order to personally see the lights. He was not disappointed:

> At twenty past eight I saw what appeared to be a ball of fire above the roof of the chapel. It came from nowhere and sprang into existence instantaneously. It seemed to be about twice the height of the chapel, about fifty feet. Suddenly it disappeared, after having lasted a minute and a half ...

Another reporter saw the lights even as he talked with Mrs. Jones in her own home. He reported to the *Barmouth Advertiser*: "Apparently a couple of miles away flashed a brilliant white light in the form of an enormous star."

On February 16th the same paper published the following report by one of its writers, Beriah G. Evans, who had accompanied Mrs. Jones to one of her services:

> Having proceeded a little over a mile along the road, all walking abreast, I saw three brilliant rays of light strike across the road from mountain to sea, throwing the stone wall twenty or thirty yards in front into bold relief, every stone plainly visible. There was not a living soul there, nor house, from which it could have come. Another half mile and a blood-red light, apparently within a foot of the ground, appeared to me in the center of the village street just before us ...

But gradually as the revival fires dimmed, as the frenzy turned to inertia, and as the townspeople emerged from the spiritual aura which had engulfed Wales, the lights—like the revival itself—burned out, leaving the mystery of their cause or source unexplained.

The Reverend A. T. Fryer, who became interested in the revival from a religious, scientific, and psychic viewpoint, was able to collect twenty-six detailed accounts from intelligent witnesses who had seen the lights or other psychic displays between 1904 and 1905. These he recorded in a lengthy paper, "Psychological Aspects of the Welsh Revival," published by the Society for Psychical Research shortly after the events had taken place.

The mysterious aerial discs made a startling comeback in 1917 in the politically and religiously shaken town of Fatima, Portugal. It is estimated that some 70,000 people—believers and skeptics alike—watched what must be considered one of the best-attested "miracles" ever.

The magic story of Fatima began in the spring of 1916. The setting was serene and simple and not a very auspicious beginning for what was eventually to become the greatest miracle in the history of Christendom. Lucia dos Santos, aged nine, Francisco Marto, aged eight, and his sister Jacinta, aged six, were tending a flock of sheep out in the fields when an overpowering radiance enveloped them. The first figure to manifest was an apparition of a man who appeared from the mist and comforted the children: "Do not fear. I am the Angel of Peace. Pray with me." After this supernatural experience the angel appeared to the children on two other occasions. Although all three children were religious Catholics, the experience had an even more profound effect on them than had their earlier training. They became more devout and even became penitents on the instructions of the figures which were to appear to them over the next several months.

The next critical day in the Fatima story was May 13, 1917, when Lucia, Francisco, and Jacinta were once more tending sheep and saw a flash of light in the sky. Hardly had they gotten over their fear that a storm was brewing than a second flash of light streaked over them. These lights heralded the first appearance of the Virgin. She stood before them, mounted atop an oak tree, shimmering in light with an aura spreading about her which illuminated the entire scene. The figure spoke to the children, urging them to continue to pray, warning them of horrible tribulations to come. The apparition warned them that they had to pray for the end of the war and later urged them to also pray for the salvation of Russia, else she would wreak havoc upon the world. Interestingly enough, on the very day this apparition appeared, Lenin had instituted the first acts of the revolution by sending horsemen into a Moscow church to destroy its altar. Several children were killed during this savage attack.

Of course, the children's parents would hear nothing of miracles. They scolded the children, punished them, and refused to allow them to revisit the oak tree at all. But the children were firm in their conviction, and soon curiosity-seekers and the devout began accompanying them to the cove to watch their communications with the invisible guardian. It was also during this period that the apparition of the Virgin Mary made the first of many personal prophecies. She promised the children that she would soon take Francisco and Jacinta to heaven with her, leaving Lucia to carry on the will of God on earth. The prophesy was fulfilled by 1920; both children died of influenza and pneumonia while still youngsters.

By the middle of July, 1917, hundreds of people were flocking to the pasture at Fatima to watch the visionary communion. The public interest in the "miracle" soon ignited the ire of government authorities. Portugal was in dire political circumstances with both the threat of world war and civil war looming over the country. The public controversy over the miracle was taken as a threat to the equilibrium of the state, so to quell the growing Fatima cult, government officials kidnapped the children and subjected them to what must be considered the most grueling ordeal since the Inquisition. At first, attempts were made to bribe the children to recant their story. They refused. Then they were threatened with imprisonment and torture. All of them, even the youngest, stayed loyal to the apparition. Finally, the chief administrator grilled each child independently, cruelly claiming that the others had been executed and that unless a confession was forthcoming, he or she too would be put to death. The children still refused, even though each had been convinced that the others had been killed. After this ordeal the administrators, in desperation, let the children go, hoping that public enthusiasm would soon wane.

Through the several months that the children had communed with the apparition, many of the onlookers also began to witness odd manifestations around the Cova do Iria during the children's raptures. On August 13, 1917, several witnesses saw orbs of light hovering near the tree, and many onlookers noticed that the tree would rustle uncannily, although there was no wind, not even a breeze. By August 19th, odd perfumed aromas pervaded the cove, and curious humming sounds were heard in the air. On September 13th, the crowd saw an aerial disc of light, much like those reported during the Welsh revival, glimmering in the sky and descending to the oak where the Virgin was said to materialize. The disc

sent out petals of light as it descended (again parallel to the orbs seen in South Wales from which sparks of light would fall), and the whole process was photographed by a Portuguese government official, Senor Antonio Robelo Martins.*
The climax of the September 17th demonstration was a proclamation which even the government officials could not ignore. The children said that the Virgin had assured them once again that on October 13th she would cause a miracle for all to see . . . a miracle to stun the world.

How was this proclamation greeted? Perhaps this is a good place to interrupt our narrative to assess the significance of the proclamation of a miracle, in order to help the reader understand the impact October 13th had on the rather diversified crowd that had traveled to Fatima either to venerate, jeer at, or embarrass the children. First, the children were in a very precarious position. They were, of course, elated at the Virgin's promise, for to them, the public miracle would be the final denouement of their spiritual quest—the conversion of the world. Nonetheless, their optimistic sentiments were more than countered by the pessimistic trepidations of their parents. Even at this date, these people did not know what to make of their children's behavior. All through the ordeal, they, along with the local clergy, had been opposed to the visions. Even now, in the face of a public miracle, they still had doubts about the spiritual authenticity of the ecstasies. They harbored a fear of which the children, in their innocence, could have had little appreciation—if no miracle transpired—and the parents had little hope that it would—the children would probably be mobbed and perhaps killed by the angry masses attending the ceremony.

Government officials were just as optimistic as the children, but for a very different reason. So far there had only been isolated reports of the lights, odors, and other telekinetic displays, and these could be easily explained as being the hallucinations of overenthusiastic superstitious onlookers. They were certain that October 13th would come and go with no miracle. The children would be discredited and the whole annoying affair could be relegated to the trash bin. So when the day did approach, the crowd gathering at the cove consisted of both those who were ardently praying for a miracle and

---

* A small book was published in France shortly after the Fatima miracle which consisted almost exclusively of photographs taken of these aerial discs and related phenomena. Copies of this book, *Fatima, Espérance du Monde* (Editions Plon), are now extremely rare.

those who were just as hopefully convinced that there wouldn't be one.

By this time too, it was clearly obvious that the children were not playing a game. Their incredible strength in the face of discouragement, punishment, and threat would have been phenomenal for an adult or even a superman. Moreover, through the children had come both personal and political prophecies which revealed acute knowledge of the world situation. Lastly, as the day grew closer, independent witnesses were seeing lights and other telekinetic displays at the cove.

October 13th finally arrived; it was the worst possible day for a miracle. It had drizzled all night, the sky was darkened by banks of clouds, and a fierce wind was blowing over the town. Despite the awful weather, thousands of people began to mass around the cove to wait for the children and the miracle. Many of them had walked all through the night, coming from miles around, and they were drenched and uncomfortable.

Avelino de Almeida, managing editor of *O Seculo*, wrote a beautiful account of the ensuing events:

> Nearly all, men and women, have bare feet, the women carrying their footgear in bags on their heads, the men leaning on great staves and carefully grasping umbrellas also. One would say that they were all oblivious to what was going on about them, with a great lack of interest in their journey and in other travelers, as if lost in a dream, reciting their Rosary in a sad rhythmic chant. A woman says the first part, the "Hail, Mary," her companions in chorus say the second part of the prayer. With sure and rhythmical steps they tread the dusty road which runs between the pine woods and the olive groves, so that they may arrive before night at the place of the apparition, where, under the severe and cold light of the stars, they hope they can sleep, keeping the first places near the blessed azinheira so that today they can see better.

Another crowd mobbed the houses in which the children slept. It was a miracle that they made it to the cove at all, as they had to push their way through the overenthusiastic crowd.

By the time the children reached the cove, it was pouring rain. The skeptics were delighted! Noontime was approaching, the hour of the prophesied miracle, and the Virgin had not yet appeared to the children. The crowd was growing restless, and the government officials had to suppress their delight at the fiasco in order to turn their attention to averting the riot which was no doubt soon to break. The tension mounted as Lucia cried out in a firm voice: "Put down your umbrellas." The crowd did so, but there still was no sight of any miracle. The children fell to their knees in prayer as Lucia finally announced that she saw the beautiful apparition. The figure beseeched the children to build a chapel, promised that the war would soon end, and that many sinners would be converted. During the proceedings, the masses watched intently as the miracle gradually unfolded.

The darkened sky suddenly became illuminated. The cloud bank parted to reveal a great shining silvery disc which the crowd first took to be the sun. Its brightness almost rivaled the brilliance of the sun as it danced in the air, swirled about, and projected flames in a dazzling array of colors to earth. The awe of the people soon turned to terror as the disc ripped itself from the heavens and plunged toward the ground in a zigzag motion. To some, the end of the world seemed near. But just as swiftly as it had descended, the orb retraced its zigzag pattern back into the sky. The sun's radiance enveloped the countryside, the storm was over, and the witnesses discovered that, even though they had been drenched with rain, they were perfectly dry.

Naturally there is some discrepancy in the many eyewitness accounts of the orb. Some claim that the disc was actually the sun, while others believe it was an independent vehicle of some sort. It is likely that the orb was honestly mistaken for the sun while actually being a huge aerial disc. Clouds had completely enveloped the sky, and the orb first appeared through an opening in them. The physical sun would have been completely obscured by clouds, so the two objects would not have been seen at the same time. As the disc ascended to the sky, the clouds broke up so that the sun's radiance probably enveloped the orb, giving the illusion that it had become, or merged with, the sun. In all respects, the Fatima miracle seems to be a spectacular version of the same type of lights seen during the Welsh revival. These lights also bounced about and moved in zigzag motions. Nor was the disc only seen at Fatima—onlookers miles away saw the display. The Portuguese poet Alfonso Lopes Vieira saw the disc from his residence in S. Pedro de Moel, forty kilometers away. In towns adjacent to Fatima, people were running about the streets shouting as they watched the strange spectacle. One witness, Father Inacio Lourenco, recounted that although twelve miles away from Fatima at the time, he, his teachers, and classmates all ran out of their school building when they heard shouts coming from the street. Looking to the skies, they saw the disc and scrutinized its odd trajectory. "It was like a globe of snow revolving on itself. Then suddenly it seemed to come down in a zigzag, threatening to fall on the earth. Terrified, I ran to shelter myself in the midst of the people. All were weeping, expecting from one moment to the next the end of the world."

When the eminent historian William Thomas Walsh decided to write a history of the miracle in the 1940s, he was able to cross-examine several witnesses from Fatima, the accounts of which were included in his *Our Lady of Fatima*, one of the best available books on the entire affair.

There can be no doubt that the phenomenon was very real, for it was seen by thousands at or around Fatima. Communities farther away reported no unusual activities in the sky, so it was obviously not the sun but some other light that caused the miracle. In trying to understand just what happened at Fatima in 1917 one must look back to the Welsh revival, for obvious parallels can be found in the accounts about the lights.

- In both cases the lights seemed linked to individuals leading the religious assemblies. They were clearly linked to Mrs. Jones in Wales and to the children at Fatima.
- In both cases the lights appeared during group religious observances as orbs of light in the air. Remember that before the October miracle at Fatima orbs of light had already been seen by the oak tree in September.
- Onlookers at both Fatima and in Wales noticed that the lights bounced, spun off flares, and moved in zigzag fashion.

There is more in common between Fatima and Wales than just the lights. The social and religious setting was also quite similar. Both in Wales and Portugal religious sentiments and emotions were brewing even before the revivals. When the revivals were underway, huge crowds engaged in dramatic religious demonstrations with the expectation that the miraculous would manifest before them. I cannot help but believe that through the collective psychic abilities of these masses a vast amount of free-floating psychic force was liberated which caused the lights. They were not miracles in the sense that they were caused by God, but they do demonstrate the unbelievable forces we harbor within our own minds and bodies.

At the beginning of the book, I stated that having confronted many psychic phenomena I know that even wilder things are possible. Perhaps now is the time to give you an example and apply it to Fatima. One evening I was visiting with my friend and colleague Mr. Raymond Bayless and a psychic with whom we have both worked, Mr. Attila von Szalay, in whose presence physical phenomena have often occurred. It was during this tête-à-tête that I was able to witness one of these spontaneous occurrences. We were sitting in a dimly lit room, and Raymond and another guest were busily trying to resolve a friendly argument; Von Szalay was distracted at the time. I happened to be looking at the floor by his foot when suddenly, an amorphous silvery orb of light about the size of a half dollar appeared by his shoe, hovered for a moment, disappeared, and reappeared a few inches farther up his leg, then vanished for good. Only von Szalay and I noticed the effect.

Now, if Mr. von Szalay can project these little orbs of light through his psychic ability, what vaster phenomena could be produced by large groups of people worked up to an emotional pitch? During poltergeist outbreaks the pent-up emotions of the family surge forth into a cyclone of psychic energy as objects are toppled, crockery thrown, and windows smashed. In some cases, psychic lights are seen as well. W. G. Roll, who is an avid poltergeist hunter as well as project director for the Psychical Research Foundation in Durham, North Carolina, investigated a poltergeist outbreak in Clayton, North Carolina, in 1962, during which flashes of light invaded the house. During religious revivals, a similar process might be taking effect. The pent-up fervor of the crowd projects outwardly into magnificent psychokinetic manifestations. The lights are the product of these projections. They are, simply stated, cosmic poltergeists.

It would be easy to end our consideration of these lights with the beautiful narrative of Fatima. But the whirling lights were to appear once more over the Iberian peninsula years later. Garabandal, Spain, was the scene of a vast religious reawakening when a group of children saw the figure of the Virgin, just as at Fatima. Here too the miraculous lights came after the revival.

The children, Jacinta, Conchita, Maria Dolores, and Mary Cruz, were all under thirteen years of age, and all had been brought up in traditional Roman Catholic families. The Garabandal miracles began innocuously enough on July 18, 1961, a holiday celebrating San Sebastian de Garabandal, the patron saint of the little town. Using the merriment and colorful celebrations as a cover, Conchita and Mary Cruz decided to engage in a little mischief. They stole away to a nearby orchard to poach a few green apples. No sooner had the girls carried out their petty theft than they heard what sounded like a gentle roll of thunder. Before them appeared what Conchita later described as "a most beautiful figure with a great deal of light, which did not at all tire my eyes."

Soon the little town was riddled with rumors and gossip about the little children who had seen the "angel." Neither the girls' parents nor the village priest were very happy about the commotion, and they tried to force the girls into recanting their story, but the children were steadfast.

The aftermath of the vision closely paralleled Fatima. Soon the two girls were joined by two others who also began seeing the figure; the four children returned to the fields to wait the appearance of the apparition, and curious crowds accompanied them. The girls fell into ecstasy for hours, gazed at the heavens, became rigid and cataleptic, or would walk about the fields impervious to anyone else. One of the most bizarre manifestations of the ecstasies was the partial levitation of two of the girls. Both Marie Dolores and Conchita would fall rigid to the ground, and slowly parts of their bodies would rise as though supported by an invisible prop. In itself, this is hardly evidence of anything supernormal, for epileptics often assume similar body postures during seizures. But in one case several witnesses swore that Conchita was lifted completely off the ground by the power of the spirit. A photograph was taken of this phenomenon from only a few feet away. The print I have seen is impressive but not convincing. Although both her legs and arms are totally levitated, Conchita's dress still dangles down, obscuring the gound, so it is impossible to verify that she is completely raised. One witness told reporters, "after she knelt down, she arched over backward until she was reclining on the floor. All at once it was as if she was lifted upward. People right around her claimed that not a single part of her was touching the floor, but I cannot testify to this because from where I stood, I couldn't be certain."

Tape recordings were made of the muttering of the children during their ecstasies as they "talked" to the apparition. Innumerable investigators poked pins into the girls or tried other harsh tests to see if they could break the cataleptic states. These attempts were uniformly unsuccessful.

On July 3, 1962, about a year after the first events at Garabandal, Conchita announced that a miracle would occur in fifteen days. Her description of exactly what was supposed to happen was obscure, but gradually it was claimed that St. Michael would appear and give Conchita communion and that part of the ceremony would be visible to any and all onlookers. As the day drew near, the villagers and visitors became restless; they waited for news that Conchita had received the "call" and had entered into one of her raptures. The call finally came in the middle of the night; Conchita stumbled out of bed, walked from her house to the adjoining street, and fell to her knees in silent prayer. As crowds began to flock around her, Conchita opened her mouth and stared upward motionless. Streaks of moonlight illuminated her figure, and then *suddenly a Host materialized on her outstretched tongue*. One witness, a French doctor, J. Coux, testified that it happened, "in a fraction of seconds—quicker than the human eye can perceive. It happened so quickly, it is hard to explain. If it was a deception, then I no longer believe in anything that happened at Garabandal."

Conchita held the Host outstretched for several minutes for all to see. After the "miracle," her raptures became less and less frequent until they ceased altogether in 1965.

I wish I could maintain that the miracle of the Host was authentic, but I cannot. It was dark, even the moon had to fight its way through the clouds, and it seems quite possible that Conchita could have had the Host in her mouth all the while and then projected it to her tongue. It is too bad that a motion picture was not made of the event, for then a frame-by-frame analysis could better pin down how and when the Host appeared. As for now, all we have are photographs of Conchita and the Host, which tell us exactly nothing about the event itself.

Despite all of the attendant publicity, no source or news accounts mentioned the aerial discs that were seen at Garabandal after the revival. The descriptions of these orbs of light are identical to the ones seen at Fatima and during the great Welsh revival. There is no information about any discs materializing during the event at Garabandal, but after the miracle, pilgrims journeying to Garabandal witnessed them. Compare the following story from the British paper, the *Sunday Express* (June 4, 1972), to the sun disc at Fatima.

> In a Spanish mountain-top village a group of British pilgrims gazed above them in awe. The evening sun seemed to

be surrounded by a aura of colours, spinning and pulsating in the sky.

Forty men and women in the party are certain they saw a miracle. The group, most strangers to each other, had travelled to the tiny village of Garabandal in northern Spain, where, in 1961, four village children had claimed to have seen the Virgin Mary and the baby Jesus.

One of the British pilgrims, Mrs. Gwendoline Hurndall, a night sister at St. Joseph's Hospital, Hackney, East London, said yesterday: "We found we could stare into the sun without sunglasses. The outline of a cross had been seen and I just saw a part of it before it vanished. Then the sun began to spin like a Catherine-wheel, first one way and then the other. Then it started to jump like a yoyo for a few minutes before going back to spinning again.

Another of the pilgrims, Miss Marina Foley, who works in a chemist's shop in Holborn, London said: "The sun looked like a flat white disc and it was spinning in a clockwise direction and pulsating to and fro."

But a psychiatrist said: "People who have travelled hundreds of miles on a pilgrimage tend to have a sense of expectation. In a high emotional state of mind anything could happen."

Another explanation could be that staring straight at the sun can fatigue the optic nerve and cause illusions.

Dr. Alan Hunter acting director of the Royal Observatory at Herstmonceux, Sussex, said: "We take photographs of the sun every day and would certainly have noticed if anything unusual had happened."

Despite Dr. Hunter's pessimism, the description of the Garabandal disc is too similar to the Fatima light to be easily dismissed. Once again, it is doubtful if the travelers actually saw the sun, but their mistaking it for the sun closely parallels the crowd reaction to the Fatima light. As the anonymous psychiatrist suggested, people in an emotional state of mind might "see" anything. All we have to do is amend this statement slightly to come up with a possible explanation for the Garabandal and Fatima lights: people in an emotional and religious frame of mind are likely to *create* almost anything. There seems to be a definite relationship between these lights and crowd activities. Although the Welsh revival lights were seen randomly during 1904-5, the most spectacular displays of high altitude disc activity occurred during mass revival demonstrations. At Fatima, thousands of people had crowded together when the lights appeared. The Garabandal light was seen collectively by a small but enthusiastic group of pilgrims.

Another bit of evidence linking these orbs to crowd activity came to my attention in a rather curious way in 1969. A friend of mine had gone to Bali for a vacation and during her stay had witnessed an impressive native ceremony. It was a religious observance complete with dancing, singing, trances, and the like. Now, whether this was a true religious ceremony or only a show that the natives put on for the tourist trade is something I don't know. But my friend swore to me that during the frenzy she saw globes of white light appear in the air above the natives as they danced.

The shimmering figures seen at Fatima and Garabandal were seen only by the children during their ecstasies. To the crowds of witnesses, whether these figures were real or imaginary was a moot point. Were they aberrations? Clairvoyant visions? Hysterical hallucinations? Or a direct contact with the Divine? A possible answer to these questions exploded onto the scene in 1968 when over a million open-mouthed spectators watched as an apparition of the Virgin appeared atop a church in Zeitoun, Egypt.

Zietoun has a spiritual heritage that ranks second only to Jerusalem and Mecca. It is a rather shabby northern suburb of Cairo, yet according to Egyptian belief it is near the spot where the Holy Family sought shelter during Herod's massacre in his search for the infant Christ. One of the larger structures in Zeitoun is the impressive Church of St. Mary. Today, seven years later, I still regret that when the accounts of the Zeitoun miracle hit the press I could not have packed off to Egypt to see the nightly apparitional displays which took place atop that church.

The figure first appeared on the night of April 2, 1968. Two mechanics were working at a nearby garage when they saw what they first mistook for a nun in white standing on top of the church's large dome. They immediately jumped to the conclusion that the nun was planning to plunge from the heights and frantically called an emergency squad. Gradually a crowd formed around the church to watch the radiant figure. For several months thereafter the apparition would appear nightly.

The Reverend Jerome Palmer, who has written the history of the appearance in his book, *Our Lady Returns to Egypt*, notes that the apparition was heralded by glowing aerial lights:

The appearances of Our Lady usually are heralded by mysterious lights. Not only does she appear in a burst of brilliant light, so bright in fact that spectators find it impossible to distinguish her features, but flashing lights (compared by some witnesses to fluorescent lights or sheet lightning) precede the appearances by some fifteen minutes. These flashes come sometimes directly above the church, sometimes in the clouds above.

The lights often jelled into the figure of the Virgin. Often odd light forms resembling birds would appear about or before her. The figure itself showed definite intelligence and would pace about the top of the church and bow to the crowd, and the whole church top began to glow with colossal light. Several astonishing photographs were taken of the apparition.

Church authorities were quick to send field representatives to look into the miracles which were being viewed nightly by hundreds of people. Bishop Athenasius was personally sent by His Holiness Pope Kyrillos VI and his report reads in part:

> The first thing we saw when we got there about 11:00 P.M. was something in the opening under the northeast dome. A silhouette, not very bright, started at the bottom of the opening and rose slowly. At first I did not see it but many people said they saw it. I began to realize it was there. It lasted for 20 minutes and then disappeared. I told the people I could not report that, if there was nothing more. We stood among the large gathering of people until 3:45 in the morning. At dawn some of those who had come with me came running from the northern street along the church and said, "The lady is over the middle dome." I was told that some clouds covered the dome, when something like fluorescent lamps began to illumine the sky. Suddenly there she was standing in full figure. I worked my way through the crowd to the front of the figure. She was five or six meters above the dome, high in the sky, full figure, like a phosphorescent statue but not so stiff as a statue, for her body and clothing moved. It was very difficult for me to stand all the time before the figure, as human waves were pushing me from all sides. One would estimate the crowd at 100,000. In an hour or so, I think I stood before the figure eight or nine times.
>
> After I left the crowd, I again heard cries from the people. I returned to the little house or office building south of the church and stood inside from four to five o'clock, looking at the figure. It never disappeared. Our Lady looked to the north; she waved her hand, she blessed the people, sometimes

in the direction where we stood. She was very quiet, full of glory.

About five minutes before five, the apparition began to grow fainter. The light gave way to a cloud, bright at first, then less and less bright until it disappeared. I went there many times later but that appearance made the greatest impression upon me.

On another night I visited the church. I took the door keys and entered, locking the doors from the inside. As I stood on the ladder that led from the second floor to the top, my eyes turned to the ceiling or inner dome. No one could see me. I was shaking all over. I took hold of the ladder. I felt there was something unusual there. I prayed: "If you are there, Holy Mary, let me see you. I just want to give witness to you."

Then I heard the people shouting. I hurried outside and saw the Virgin standing one meter from where I had been.

The figure would often appear, disappear, and reappear for hours. On May 5, 1968, she appeared before thousands of spectators for eight hours. Sometimes only a disc of light would be seen above the church, from which the form would materialize. One witness told Reverend Palmer:

The most wonderful scene occurred under the northeast dome, above the icon of Our Lady on the feast of the Flight of the Holy Family, June 1. About 9:00 or 9:30 at night a light appeared in the center of the opening beneath the small dome. The light took the shape of a sphere, moving up and down. Then slowly it moved out through the supporting archway and took the form of St. Mary. It lasted two or three minutes, and as usual the people shouted to her. She usually acknowledges their greetings with both hands, or with one, if she should be holding the olive branch of the Christ Child. She seems happy and smiling, always kind, but somewhat sad. She then returned to the dome and the figure became again a round ball of light and gradually faded into the darkness.

The many photographs taken of the Zeitoun miracle include several of the figure itself shimmering in a dazzling whiteness. In another photograph her brilliant aura is spread over the church dome which can be seen radiating the same type of glow. Other snapshots show the figure *floating* above the church, and one photograph caught the birdlike objects hovering near her. The Zeitoun case is probably the most impressive and well-documented "miracle" in modern times.

Mysteries and Miracles

The apparition appeared continually for several months until the Egyptian government tried to cash in on the miracle. They cleared a spectators' area below the church and began charging an admission fee. Almost as if in conscious protest, the figure gradually appeared less and less often but nonetheless continued to materialize until 1971.

The Zeitoun case is the ultimate unfolding of the same force which was no doubt present at Fatima, Garabandal, and Wales. The flashing lights and orbs at Zeitoun seem to have been the outcome of a "building-up" process, a gradual process of psychic materialization which culminated in the apparition. Could the Fatima and Wales lights have been abortive attempts at a similar miracle? The whole area of Zeitoun is saturated by a spiritual presence. One can almost feel the devotion of Egyptian Christians in memory of the Holy Family's flight, their intense religious nature, and the holy traditions associated with the site. Over the centuries could it be possible that those thoughts and emotions have impressed upon the church a *psychic blueprint* of the Holy Family? In other words, could those who have come to Zeitoun over the years in veneration gradually have built up a living presence of the Virgin formed from some lingering and continually fed psychic force liberated through their prayers and observances? Perhaps in 1968 the force finally gained sufficient strength to burst forth for all to see.

The topic that I have carefully avoided discussing so far is one that might be obvious. One cannot overlook for long the relationship of these aerial discs and acrobatics to UFO activity. Let's reexamine the disc seen at Fatima, Zeitoun, Wales, and Garabandal and compare them to what we know about UFOs. There are some direct parallels:

1. During the Welsh revival large lights were seen surrounded by smaller subsidiary lights. This description sounds suspiciously like reports of several UFOs that have been seen to flock around a larger vehicle. This has led to the concept of "mother ships."

2. The lights in Wales and at Fatima dissolved into or gave off puffs of smoke. UFO witnesses have noted that UFOs often spontaneously disappear, leaving only a trail of smoke or vapor behind.

3. The Welsh lights were seen to blink on and off. This is often mentioned by UFO-sighters, many of whom even believe that the blinking represents attempts at communication.

4. The lights in Wales, Fatima, and Garabandal moved in what witnesses described as a "zigzag" trajectory. UFO witnesses have also seen these vehicles hover, quiver, and then zigzag away at incredible speeds.

5. At Fatima, the appearance of the figure was accompanied by "humming" sounds. One of the most commonly reported sounds heard coming from UFOs, or which drew the witnesses' attention to them, are sounds described variously as "whizzing," "buzzing," "humming," or "whirling."

A detailed comparison of the Fatima orb to UFO observation was made by Paul Thomas in his book *Flying Saucers Through the Ages*. He found seven direct points of similarity.

1. The Fatima disc was a flat, shining, but not overly brilliant disc. UFOs are also often disc-like. One UFO witness Thomas quoted described what he saw as "a luminous disc as large as the full moon, but shining with a brighter glow."

2. The Fatima light glowed softly. UFOs are also known not so much to project or shine light, but to glow like neon.

3. As we noted earlier, the Fatima disc revolved and swirled about at high speed. UFOs engage in the same type of acrobatic activity.

4. The Fatima light radiated flares of multicolored lights. UFOs are also multicolored and will frequently change color as they move.

5. The Fatima light zigzagged, a trajectory which seems to be a common trait of these "religious lights." UFOs maneuver similarly.

6. After the Fatima light plunged to the ground, it quickly ascended back into the sky. Thomas quotes a similar account of a UFO sighting in which the orb spun to the ground and "... after hanging for a moment like a pendulum, the craft shot upward at an angle, and disappeared."

7. The clothes of the onlookers were completely dry after the miracle despite the rain. In a few UFO cases it has been noted that the ground is found to be inexplicably dry after the craft has flown overhead, despite the fact that natural moisture or rain had saturated the area earlier.

The comparison made by Thomas between the Fatima light and UFO reports and my own more general list of comparisons made previously point in a single direction. There appears to be little doubt that *some* UFO activity is of the same nature and source as the revival discs. It is also clear to me that the lights seen at Fatima, Wales, Garabandal, and

Zeitoun were psychic projections of almost unbelievable magnitude. With all this in mind, we can't avoid confronting the next million dollar question—Are UFOs space vehicles or psychic entities?

CHAPTER 4

UFOs: Space Vehicles or Psychic Entities?

Kim and Janice were driving home after a date. It was late and the two New England students just wanted to get home. As they drove down an infrequently traveled byway, Janice spotted an object in the sky. Startled, she pointed out the odd light to Kim, who pulled the car over; it stalled before he could turn off the ignition, and the lights and radio faded out ominously. Kim frantically tried to start the car, but to all intents and purposes the engine was dead. However, the car had become only a secondary concern by then, for, as Kim and Janice sat petrified, the odd light advanced toward them. The object was too large to be a plane; it had moved in the same direction as the car, yet it made no sound nor did it affect the street lights in the area. When it darted off an instant later, the automobile started easily.

Mr. Yves Prigent was about to sit down to lunch at his office in the Oloron High School faculty quarters. He had been joined by Mme. Prigent and their three children. Just as they were about to sit down to enjoy their meal, one of the children, standing at a northern window, cried out, "Oh, Papa, come look, it's fantastic." The whole family scurried to the window and saw a strange cloudlike object floating silently in the air. It was cylindrical in shape and inclined at about a 45-degree angle. Prigent estimated that it was floating about two or three kilometers from the ground. The object appeared whitish, and puffs of smoke were ejected from its upper side. To his amazement, M. Prigent realized that several similar objects were hovering in front of the one that had first caught his attention, and all were following the same trajectory. Actually the solid objects were moving by pairs in a zig-zag path. As the pairs split up, a whitish lightning-like streak

UFOs: Space Vehicles or Psychic Entities? 81

appeared between them. As the crafts flew off, the whitish substance fell from them, littering the ground, trees, and town roofs. The substance gradually dissipated. Ten days later, this same aerial exhibition was repeated over a nearby town.

On a typical sunny July afternoon in 1945, Raymond Bayless was working for the Firestone Tire and Rubber Company in downtown Los Angeles when the tedium of the day's work was interrupted by the shouts of a fellow worker. He had been on the roof and rushed in shouting that "fireballs" were catapulting from the sky. Since this employee was endearingly known as "Rum-dumb McNab," his story was not greeted with too much excitement. But McNab was so insistent that Bayless climbed atop the East 8th Avenue building and looked northward. To his surprise, he saw brilliant orange darts of light appear from one point in the sky and plunge earthward, whitish smoke pouring out behind them. They all followed the same path, but some would stop in their plunge, reverse themselves, and fly back to the point of origin and disappear. The objects continued their heavenly acrobatics for several hours, yet no report of the phenomenon was ever made over the radio or in the newspapers.

Seven years later, on September 19, 1952, a silver disc shot over several naval vessels which were taking part in a NATO exercise in the North Sea. Wallace Litwin, a press reporter aboard the *Franklin Roosevelt*, photographed the disc. According to Lieutenant John W. Kilburn, the object was a metal disc that gradually reduced speed, fluttered like a leaf, revolved like a top, and then shot off at an incredible speed before disappearing westward. The entire event lasted only twenty seconds or so.*

All of the people involved in these incidents saw phenomena that we usually lump together as "UFOs," which is short for "unidentified flying objects." The term "UFO" offers no theory as to what the objects are, but has generally become synonymous with "flying saucers." However, the UFO problem is not that simple. Each of the four cases I have just cited represents very unique aspects of the UFO phenomenon. One UFO was only a light in the sky, but powerful enough to kill a car engine; another was a disc, yet another was cylindrical in shape, and Bayless' UFO was a fiery orb of light, yet all can be called UFOs.

* These four cases have been quoted from J. Allen Hynek's *The UFO Experience*, Aime Michel's *The Truth about Flying Saucers*, and Raymond Bayless' *Experiences of a Psychical Investigator*.

There is no such thing as a typical UFO encounter. Each report is unique since the UFO mystery encompasses a vast panorama of different effects. For example, Mr. Brown is driving in the country when he sees a glittering light in a nearby field. Sparked by curiosity and a dash of bravery, he gets out of his car, peeks from behind some bushes, and sees a saucerlike object resting clandestinely in a deserted pasture. He also sees four silver-clad, four-foot tall occupants collecting grass samples around it. Mr. Smith, on the other hand, wakes up one night and hears a voice in his head say, "Get up and look out your window." He does so and sees a UFO flying overhead. Mr. Jones is awakened by the barking of his dogs. He slips on a bathrobe, bolts out to his backyard, and sees a squadron of UFOs flying overhead. His dogs cower by the garage. Mr. Jones becomes transfixed as "alien thoughts" bombard his mind. Two weeks later, both Jones and his wife hear footsteps around their home, household objects disappear and reappear in odd places, and their pets behave oddly, growling or shivering in fear for no apparent reason.

The above hypothetical examples are stereotyped from actual UFO accounts. The study of UFOs is no longer merely one of figuring out if an object seen in the sky is a weather balloon, helicopter, light projection, or—if all else fails—a genuine UFO. UFOs represent a wider mystery. It is quite common for witnesses to feel that they have made telepathic contact with UFOs or suddenly find themselves plagued by psychic experiences. As veteran Ufologist Jacques Vallee has stated in his recent book, *The Invisible College*, "No theory of UFOs can be deemed acceptable if it does not account for the reported psychic effects produced by these objects." He's dead right. There is a very significant relationship between UFOs and psychic phenomena which Ufologists and parapsychologists have ignored for years. Ufologists are now beginning to take an interest in these reports, but by and large, parapsychologists are absolutely horrified by the thought that UFOs may help us understand psi. (I only know two American parapsychologists who have any background in Ufology.) On the other hand, most Ufologists have a very poor background in parapsychology. This is indeed unfortunate, for as I will show in this chapter, UFOs might actually be psychic materializations, just as the Welsh revival and Fatima lights probably were.

At the present time, even the experts disagree greatly as to what UFOs actually are. Were you to ask, "What are UFOs

UFOs: Space Vehicles or Psychic Entities?

and where do they come from?" the answer would depend on who you asked!

Retired Air Force Major Donald E. Keyhoe stated his opinion quite explicitly when he titled his book, *Flying Saucers from Outer Space*. Keyhoe represents the mainstream of thought that UFOs are spacecraft from alien worlds surveying our little insignificant planet.

Brinsley Le Poer Trench, chairman of Contact, which is one of the world's largest UFO organizations, is also convinced that UFOs are craft. Unlike Keyhoe, however, he believes that, "... many of the UFOs come from invisible universes." Trench's belief was echoed by Ivan Sanderson, who stated in a *Psychic Observer* interview:

> It's been known to authorities for forty years now that they do not come to us through our space time. They don't come from another planet. They come through from another set of dimensions, not another dimension or a fourth dimension, but they come from *another whole universe,* or a whole bunch of universes which are interlocked with ours either in space or time. That's why we can't catch one, because they are not really there. They're like projections, but they are three-dimensional and solid objects ...

Despite these noble words, Sanderson had his own pet theory about where the UFOs come from. After analyzing hundreds of accounts, he finally concluded that "... over 50 percent of all so-called sightings of UFOs have occurred over, coming from, going away over, or plunging into or coming out of water." Thus, he concluded, " .. there is an underwater 'civilization' (or civilizations) on this planet that has been here for a very long time and which was evolved here..." and which is responsible for the UFOs.

An even more bizarre terrestrial theory about the origins of UFOs is given by Raymond Bernard in his book *The Hollow Earth*. Bernard would have us believe that "... The conception of a hollow earth ... offers the most reasonable theory of the origin of the flying saucers and far more logical than the belief in their interplanetary origin. For this reason, leading flying saucer experts ... have accepted the theory of their subterranean origin."

So, four different experts have four different solutions for the UFO mystery. As the thoughtful reader may have discerned by comparing these theories to the four accounts which opened this chapter, the same error is compounded by all of the theorists. They all assume that UFOs have but one source and have tried to figure out a unified explanation for all of them. But is this necessarily true? Couldn't there be many different types of UFOs?

None of these theories takes into account the evidence that UFOs might be intrinsically related and connected to the people who view them, and not independent objects at all. In other words, even though UFOs are physical objects, they might be projections from our own minds. There is a large body of evidence with which we can support this theory.

The first area of evidence which supports my theory that, by and large, UFOs are psychic manifestations comes from the fact that UFOs often mock our very thoughts. This would indicate that during a UFO encounter, the object is not independent of the viewers who see it or the culture in which it materializes. Here are two cases in point, both of which were reported by Ivan Sanderson who had an absolute penchant for bumping into UFOs. This is rather strange, since most people go through life without even seeing one of them, but Sanderson just kept running into them time after time. This could not be accidental, nor do I believe that Sanderson was being singled out by UFO intelligences. It seems more likely that he was actually producing the UFOs himself.

The first case stems from the agonizing years of the Second World War when Sanderson was involved in counter-espionage operations in the Caribbean. The Germans had become daring. Their submarines were surfacing in broad daylight and even signaled each other with lights. German shore parties also signaled each other with battery-powered lights. It was during this time, while Sanderson was aboard a spyship, that he noticed a bright green star overhead. Suddenly the star grew larger, lit up the entire sky, and exploded. The odd color of the star reminded Sanderson of a similar UFO that had been reported by a regiment of British soliders on the island of Curaçao. Described by them as a peacock-green, the UFO flew from the sky onto the road just ahead of the soldiers before darting out of sight. In each case, the UFO resembled the lights used by the Nazi signalers. Consequently, when Sanderson reported the incident to his superiors in London, he received a return communication stating: "Kindly desist, repeat desist, reporting green lights and other aerial phenomena and proceed with assigned duties."

It seems that green lights had started popping up all over

UFOs: Space Vehicles or Psychic Entities?

the place. They appeared in the sky, zigzagged in true UFO fashion, and as Sanderson admits:

> Not only did these things manoeuvre, they made sudden stops and starts and inexplicable angular turns. What is more, among the cays and islands they behaved exactly as did the Nazi signalers, even blinking in complex phased rhythms so that we had at first become convinced we were on to some kind of code. Finally, we experienced them both coming down from the sky and going up into it, and apparently at unbelievable speeds to boot.

Just what were these lights? In one respect they were typically UFO-ish. They hovered, cruised at high speeds, and maneuvered in angular trajectories. This indicates to me that these UFOs were actually created by the thoughts of those who, like Sanderson, were engaged in tracking down the Nazi signalers. Doesn't it seem odd that UFOs that mimicked the German lights were most often reported by those persons actively occupied in tracking them down? When Sanderson saw the starlike UFO, was it actually an independent entity or a psychic reflection from his mind?

Sanderson had another UFO encounter years later. Here too the unusual circumstances surrounding the sighting indicate that the UFO had a symbiotic connection to Sanderson's mind.

The date was July 31, 1966. Sanderson, Mrs. E. C. who was a skeptic about UFOs, John Keel who is a UFO expert, and another friend had just come home from an outing and were walking in the garden of Sanderson's home. The hour was late. Mrs. E. C., who, as we have stated, was a skeptic, had had to endure an entire evening of UFO talk over the dinner table. Suddenly she cried out, "What's that?" and pointed to a spot above Sanderson's house. There, indeed, was a UFO-like light passing overhead, traveling faster than any known terrestrial craft. Sanderson ran into his house, grabbed a pair of powerful binoculars, and zeroed in on the object. He could see that it was a solid oval that changed colors before disappearing.

Here we have a curious set of "coincidences." The topic of the evening had been UFOs. The conversation had doubtlessly been a bit constrained by the presence of a skeptic, and then the evening was climaxed by an almost classic UFO sighting right over Sanderson's home. Coincidence just isn't that neat. What are the probabilities that a UFO expert who has just spent an entire evening discussing the phenomenon in the company of a skeptic will see a UFO that very night flying right over his house? Once again, it seems very probable that the UFO was directly related to Sanderson's activities and thoughts that evening. In other words, he created it.

The fact that Sanderson kept bumping into UFOs is another telling point about the origins of these enigmas. The books of UFO experts like Sanderson and John Keel are liberally sprinkled with accounts of personal encounters with these aerial beasts. Of course, if one spends considerable time investigating UFO flaps and cases, one is bound to encounter a UFO now and then, but Sanderson's and Keel's encounters often seem to be totally spontaneous. While it would be impossible to figure out the statistical odds for the likelihood of Mr. A. seeing five UFOs in his lifetime and Mr. B. seeing none, the penchant certain people have for running into UFOs is something that needs explaining.

This all leads to another point. As I began to study Ufology as a by-product of my interest in parapsychology, I soon realized, on the basis of official UFO reports, that *if a person sees a UFO once it is highly likely he will see one again at some time during his life.*

One multi-experience UFO witness was an elderly woman who lived alone on a farm in the French Pyrenees. She began seeing lights off in the distance around the countryside in 1966. Later, other inhabitants in the community saw these spherical UFOs, which came either singly or grouped in squadrons. Six months later, the UFOs returned and seemed to single out certain witnesses, as though tracking them. One witness testified that he saw one of the orblike UFOs on his farm and that it *followed* him as he walked, and stopped the moment he did. Gradually he saw six UFOs congregating, and five days later the witness's son saw additional UFOs near the house. (This whole case was investigated and published in the September–October 1970, issue of the *Flying Saucer Review*.)

There are many accounts on record that tell of people who have seen UFOs while driving, and who have then hurried home scared to death by the incident. Subsequently, they have seen UFOs near their homes either later that same day or perhaps a few days after the initial experience. Are these people being tracked by UFOs or are they creating them, in much the same way as I believe the Welsh revival and Fatima lights were created by those who viewed them?

UFOs: Space Vehicles or Psychic Entities?

Another problem that faces proponents of the space-vehicle theory is the fact that UFOs, although they often seem to resemble aircraft, do not behave like machines. In fact, they act in reverse fashion. First of all, they seem very much like animals. They travel in "schools," play hopscotch or leapfrog, and are very sensitive to atmospheric disturbances, which prompt an increase in their appearances. (Deep-sea fish will surface similarly when there is oceanic turbulence.) Even a United States Air Force release issued in 1949 stated that, "Many of the objects described acted more like animals than anything else." Kenneth Arnold, whose famous 1947 sighting prompted our current interest in UFOs and who inadvertently coined the term "flying saucer," came to conclude that UFOs were actually space animals. This theory was most thoroughly developed by the Countess Zoe Wassilko-Serecki, an Austrian entrepreneur of the paranormal, who believed that they survived on energy.

Secondly, UFOs seem to have the ability to change shape. One would hardly expect this from a physical object. A gigantic UFO, seen over the Atlantic in 1954, actually shrank in size as it hovered. A UFO was seen over Whitly Island in October, 1963, and the report reads that the airplane-wing shaped craft, "suddenly shrank considerably in size and tilted so that its rear portion dipped into the ground." In another case, Captain Jose Lemos Ferreira, of the Portuguese services, saw a UFO during a routine practice on September 4, 1957. It expanded to over five times its initial size and then crumbled inward and disappeared. There are also many eyewitness reports that saucer-shaped objects suddenly transformed into cigarlike shapes, and vice versa.

Thirdly, if UFOs are craft, they certainly have eluded our grasp. No one has ever downed one, shot off a part of one, or captured one on the ground.

None of these facts is consistent with the theory that UFOs are physical space vehicles. But they do fit neatly into the hypothesis that they are psychic materializations—physical objects created psychically by our own minds and molded by our own will.

UFOs may not be dependent on any one person's psychic projection, as Sanderson's encounters would suggest. They often mimic a cultural aptitude. In other words, our entire culture may be projecting UFOs psychically. In the last chapter, I cited considerable evidence that groups of people might project a collective psychic force to create what can best be called "miracles." A similar explanation might exist for UFOs. It was the great psychoanalyst C. G. Jung, in his famous little book *Flying Saucers: A Modern Myth of Things Seen in the Sky*, who eloquently argued, from a purely psychological standpoint, that UFOs represent the manifestation of a cultural need. Jung did not believe that they were objective craft darting about the skies, but rather that they existed in the minds of those who saw them. Thus, they became a psychic reality. The UFOs, according to Jung, were projections reflecting a general unrest among mankind—a literal "call to the heavens" in our chaotic times.

I believe that Jung made two errors in his argument. To begin with, UFOs are at least semiphysical. They are objectively and collectively seen, they have been photographed, and have even left remnants behind, such as burned grass or fungus-like waste. Secondly, Jung was preoccupied solely with our modern interest in UFOs, which began in the late 1940s after Kenneth Arnold's Mt. Rainier sighting. But UFOs have been reported for centuries.

Nonetheless, despite the flaws in Jung's rationale, he was telling us something very important about UFOs: that *we* are creating them and that *we* have a cultural need for their appearance. The fact that they have materialized in other cultures and in other times as real objects does not force us to overhaul Jung's views too substantially. Simply recognizing that man has a vast psychic potential locked within him completes the gaps in Jung's theory.

This all leads to my next premise: *UFOs reflect the cultural needs and expectations of the society in which they appear.* This too is more consistent with a psychic rather than an interstellar explanation. If we look back into history, we find that over the years UFOs have changed in appearance to better fit into the technology of the times. In fact, they even mimic soon-to-be-made aeronautical advances. This peculiar fact was initially expounded by Brinsley Le Poer Trench in his book *Mysterious Visitors*. As he catalogued the old cases, Trench found that UFOs have progressed in appearance in line with new developments in air transportation. There are four stages of this progression in modern times.

The first progression began around the turn of the century during the famous UFO flap of 1896-97, which spread over the country and even the world. These UFOs were zeppelin-like or cigar-shaped objects, although zeppelins were not flown until a few years later. Additional sightings occurred in 1909 in England and later over New Zealand.

Many UFO authors have tried to figure out an explanation for the 1896 flap. Some believe that there was a secret network of scientists who had developed airpower before it was "officially" discovered. Others believe that it was caused by an alien race that was trying to disguise its antics by conforming to earthly technology. But in any event, these objects have all the earmarks of being typical UFOs. They were even inhabited. Although many hoaxes came out of these flaps, there were also some worthwhile reports. Here is one account from 1896 which appeared in the *Sacramento Bee:*

> Last evening between the hours of six and seven o'clock, in the year of our Lord 1896, a most startling exhibition was seen in the skies in this city of Sacramento. People standing on the sidewalks at certain points in the city between the hours stated, saw coming through the sky over the housetops what appeared to them to be merely an electric lamp propelled by some mysterious force. It came out of the east and sailed unevenly toward the southeast, dropping now nearer the earth, and now suddenly rising into the air again ...

Witnesses who were able to get a good view of the object described it as a huge cigar-shaped craft with four wings attached to its metal frame. Literally hundreds of people saw these UFOs during the outbreak. They flew over cities, hunters chanced upon them in forests, and fishermen spied them on beaches. Remember, this was four years *before* the similarly shaped zeppelins actually flew! (An excellent summary of this great airship mystery is given in Jerome Clark's and Loren Coleman's *The Unidentified.*)

Even after the development of the zeppelin, the cigar-shaped UFOs continued to appear. A description of one seen in 1909 over England reads:

> The 1907 airship was a dark, cigar-shaped object carrying a rather bright "searchlight." Like its 1897 predecessor, it is the behavior and not the appearance of the airship that connects it with modern UFO phenomenon ...

Now, there is no record or evidence in 1909 that zeppelins were ever flown in New Zealand. Yet in that year there were many reports from that island of phantom torpedo-shaped air vessels which were *identical* to the reports that came from the United States in 1896–7.

The second rung of the UFO-progression ladder came about 1910–30 when reports started to come in about mystery airplanes. Veteran UFO investigator John Keel has collected several accounts of these sightings which he wrote up in a series of articles, "Mystery Airplanes of the 1930s" in the *Flying Saucer Review*. The UFOs came out of the skies, whirring their motors, flying at very high speeds, and gradually taking on the shape of aircraft as they came into eye range. Yet they flew in places and at angles inaccessible or impossible for the craft of the day. Like the UFOs seen in 1896–7 the planes often had searchlights in front of them. The most impressive evidence for the existence of these UFOs came from Scandinavia where they were seen or tracked during weather conditions that would absolutely prohibit conventional flying. According to Keel, the Scandinavian countries were very worried about these objects since they had no identification marks on them. English pilots were nonplussed that the mystery planes could never be downed or tracked from the air.

The third rung of the progression came in 1946. Now phantom missiles had outdated the phantom airplanes! Even the French paper *Le Figaro* reported:

> More than two thousand ghost rockets have been reported during the past few months over Sweden . . . They are the subject of jokes on the music-hall stage, but the Swedish and Danish military staffs are taking the matter seriously, and have begun to investigate . . .

Like most UFOs, the rockets traveled at unbelievable speeds, both slow and fast; they were cigar-shaped and made no noise. These behavioral traits are almost identical to the antics of modern-day UFOs. Although UFOs have modified their facade over the decades, they do not seem to have changed their behavior. And old and modern UFOs alike have tended to come in waves.

Brinsley Trench took all of these facts and came up with a set of conclusions: (1) the 1896–7 and 1909 incidents came as we began to develop zeppelins; (2) the 1930s flap occurred as Western society began to develop aircraft; (3) the 1946 events seemed to echo the development of jet missiles and rockets.

Trench came to believe that perhaps an alien civilization

UFOs: Space Vehicles or Psychic Entities?

has been "seeding" information to the human race which has helped us in the development of air flight. However, let's take a psychic look at this progression of UFO shapes. In each of the critical periods, Western society was about to make technological breakthroughs in air flight. If we are, in fact, creating UFOs from our minds, wouldn't these objects tend to mimic either extant, developed, or even future or drawing-board model aircraft? To me, the great flaps of 1896, 1930, 1946, etc., represent a cultural psychic reflection from the scientific and technological consciousness of society. But could UFOs actually mimic the secret or little-known designs of soon-to-be-developed aircraft? Why not? Couldn't this collective psychic force employ ESP or precognition?

So far, I have analyzed two constituents of the UFO mystery which lead me to believe that UFOs are the creation of our own minds. First, UFOs appear in settings and at such times as to bear significantly on the life or predicament of the viewer, and some people are actually UFO-prone (Ivan Sanderson is a case in point). Secondly, UFOs have a habit of mimicking our cultural development. There are, however, even more direct link-ups between UFOs, psychic phenomena, and our minds. If UFOs are psychic materializations, then psychic outbreaks or incidents should occur when they appear. And this is exactly what we *do* find.

Now, although a few investigators have considered the psychic components in UFO reports, by and large Ufologists do not seem well versed in parapsychology. For example, one Ufologist suggested that Betty and Barney Hill (the famous couple who claimed that they were taken aboard a flying saucer and later under hypnosis independently told exactly the same story) had not been aboard a spacecraft at all but that one of the team telepathically transferred the story to the other's brain. Now anyone well versed in parapsychology would realize that this explanation is pretty outlandish. From years of investigations and laboratory work we know that ESP is a very inaccurate information channel. In fact, it is so bad as to be useless. Telepathically transferred or assimilated information is usually fragmented, symbolic, or distorted. There is no such thing as "perfect" ESP. So to theorize that two people could come out with carbon-copy stories as a result of telepathic infection runs completely counter to everything that parapsychology has uncovered about the faculty.

When we talk about psychic phenomena, we are referring

to two types of effects: *ESP*, which would entail telepathy, clairvoyance, and precognition; and *psychokinesis*, the movement of matter or influence over matter by the human will. These phenomena represent contacts with the enviroment which are not due to any known or inferrable sensory or physical channel. The words "or inferrable" are very important. If Mr. A. looks at his wife, who thereupon goes to the corner of their living room and gets him his favorite pipe, this is not necessarily ESP. I can *infer* that Mr. A. shot a glance at his pipe, and his wife, seeing the motion, understod what he wanted through no words were actually spoken. Now, if Mr. A. and Mrs. A. were separated in two different rooms, that would be another matter altogether! On the other hand, if I see Mr. A. wave his hand over a pencil and the object responds and rolls along paralleling his motion for a few inches, I can *infer* that Mr. A. has set up an electrostatic field by any one of several normal and explainable means.

Because many writers on the UFO problem do not realize that what they claim to be a paranormal phenomenon is really nothing of the sort, there has been quite a bit of very confused writing about the interrelationship between UFOs and psychic phenomena. One of the first attempts to find paranormal concomitants to UFO reports was made by Trench in his *Mysterious Visitors*. He attributes the following paranormal powers and manifestations to the UFOs: teleportation, levitation, materialization, animal ESP, telepathic interaction with witnesses, and so forth. This is pretty varied fare, yet very little of it is paranormal in the true parapsychological sense. Take, for example, the following cases:

If a UFO is seen flying overhead, hovers over a horse in a pasture and lifts it up, this is not true levitation. (This actually did happen according to a humorous twentieth-century UFO case.) It is likely that some physical force was used to propel the animal. Likewise, if a UFO suddenly vanishes in thin air, we cannot say it "dematerialized" since we don't have much evidence that the object was ever there *physically* in the first place. If a witness sees a UFO and suddenly finds his head filled with strange thoughts or even communications, there is no way of discerning if these are delusions or true telepathic messages. When animals react bizarrely before a UFO appears, is this precognition or just typical animal sensitivity to high-frequency sounds that elude our own ears?

Even veteran Ufologists make these same mistakes. Although Jacques Vallee is a leading exponent of a new school

UFOs: Space Vehicles or Psychic Entities?

of Ufology which is trying to bridge the gap between UFOs and psychic phenomena, he falls into the same trap in his otherwise pioneering book, *The Invisible College*. He writes:

> In recent years, too, the report of paranormal events in connection with close encounters with UFOs seems to have become the rule rather than the exception and most investigators have found it very difficult to deal with this aspect of the cases. Such events might take the form of minor 'unexplained coincidences" in which a man might have had a dream prior to the sightings (or heard a knock on the door and gone to open it, only to find no one was there, as happened to a policeman who later the same evening reported being paralyzed by two occupants of an unknown craft). Sometimes the event was more significant. A number of witnesses, for example, reported perceiving distinct 'messages' inside their heads, a fact they interpreted as an indication of a telepathic ability on the part of the UFO occupants. Still other categories of psychic events are the distortions of time and space reported by witnesses, the apparent violations of physical laws represented by the sudden appearance and dissappearance of physical craft. . . .

Here again, much of what Dr. Vallee talks about cannot be properly defined as psychic. Distortions of space-time continuums, being invaded by alien thoughts, etc., may be delusions or manipulations of natural laws. But there is no way of proving that these were nonsensory experiences or experiences which transcend physical laws.

Nonetheless, there are very definite psychic components to UFO sightings. Three phenomena stand out predominantly, and they serve as the second line of evidence that UFOs are structured from psychic forces:

1. Some people have seen UFOs after receiving extrasensory impressions as to where to look or when to watch for them.

2. People who see UFOs sometimes report psychokinetic disturbances in their homes or become centers of full-fledged poltergeist activity.

3. UFO witnesses sometimes find themselves miraculously healed of physical problems or even degenerative illnesses.

Let's take a look at these unusual case reports in turn and judge the true psychic components of UFO sightings. The interrelationship between extrasensory preception and UFO encounters is a complex one. In the following cases the witnesses all felt or implied that somehow their encounters were not by chance, but that they were directed, willed, or influenced psychically to the spot where they could see the UFO. The following example, reported by Mr. D. P. Daish of Bedfordshire, England, is typical:

> On 16th January, 1974, around 2300 hours I was at home in the kitchen making myself a drink when I felt the urge to go and look outside the back door. The night was a wild one; at least for this part of the country, with a strong gale . . . the sky was partly cloudy with low clouds and excellent visibility . . . To the northwest I saw a red light, almost as bright as the brightest star or planet in the sky, moving in a most peculiar manner. The best way I can describe the motion is to compare it with that of a ping-pong ball on a jet of water, that is, moving up and down very rapidly and erratically. I was puzzled, to say the least, and hurried back inside to call my mother and my brother to come and look . . . The light appeared to be quite close, as far as I could tell in the circumstances, approximately over the Old Warden Aerodrome, where a number of antique aircraft are kept and flown on suitable occasions. We watched the light weaving and bobbing for about ten minutes, then it suddenly dropped like a stone and disappeared from sight . . .*

The remark made by Mr. Daish that he "felt the urge to go and look outside the back door" smacks of ESP. Daish gives no rational explanation as to *why* he was prompted to interrupt his activities to look outside, yet his illogical act led him right into a UFO observation. Is this coincidence or something more?

The vast majority of cases of telepathically induced UFO sightings fall into this category. The witness rarely realizes that he is actively being influenced but instead more often finds himself carrying out inexplicable actions which lead him directly into the path of a UFO. For example, compare Mr. Daish's account with the following brief reports (italics are mine):

> My family and I were on holiday on the Norfolk Broads. Four of us were playing about with a football *when suddenly all four of us looked almost vertically upwards for no apparent reason.* A fraction of a second later, an object appeared. It was three or four times ar large as a star and bright orange in colour. In the next instant it disappeared, and reappeared ninety degrees from its first position. This is

---

* This case and the two cases that follow have been abridged from longer reports which appeared in the correspondence column of the *Flying Saucer Review*, Vol. 21, No. 1, 1975.

all we saw, but it worried us slightly. *We couldn't understand why we had all looked up at the same instant.*

The narrator of this report goes on to tell of another UFO sighting he made about three years later. This fits into the pattern I outlined earlier: a person who sees one UFO is likely to see another one sometime later in his life.

The following report from a London widow falls into this same ESP pattern. She too was witness to a UFO flight, and her report strongly suggests that the experience was prompted by ESP:

> On that morning (January 28, 1975) at 6:15, *I awoke suddenly after only five hours sleep, wondering what had roused me.* After paying a visit to the bathroom without switching any lights on at all, as I fully intended to return to bed, I went to my kitchen window for a brief glimpse of the weather. It was very dark and overcast ... my eyes were drawn to a huge globe of light in the sky between a hundred and two hundred feet above the trees. It was absolutely stationary, pulsating with a brilliant, pale golden light. I stood observing it for at least three minutes ... Without taking my eyes off it, I began to wonder how long I should stand there rationalizing this strange phenomenon, when suddenly it moved silently and swiftly in a straight line westward along the horizon, the light growing smaller as it went into the distance. I had it in sight for eight to ten seconds before it disappeared.

Being awakened from sleep just in time to see a UFO seems to be a common report. In the above case, the witness wondered *why* she awoke and thus implies that this interruption was an unusual variant of her sleep habits. Her report is similar to the one which preceeds it, in which the narrator wondered why he and his companions looked to the skies for no apparent reason just in time to see a UFO overhead. The relationship between ESP and sleep is an intriguing one. Parapsychologists who have collected cases of spontaneous ESP have long known that a majority of cases occur when the person is asleep and usually dreaming. Just take a look at the following statistics. Dr. Louisa Rhine of the Institute for Parapsychology of the Foundation for Research on the Nature of Man, in Durham, N. C., has been collecting cases of spontaneous ESP for several years, and her analyses of these cases have appeared over the years in the *Journal of Parapsychology*. She found that 58 percent of her cases occurred through dreams when the subjects were asleep. A German parapsychologist, G. Sannwald, carried out an analysis of 1,000 cases he had collected in his country and found 63 percent were cases of dream ESP. In a similar study in India, 52.4 percent of the cases occurred during sleep. It would seem that we are more receptive to ESP during sleep when our minds are not occupied by day-to-day distractions or by a barrage of high-priority sensory experiences. It appears that ESP signals might be better able to "get through" when we are asleep. At Maimonides Medical Center in Brooklyn, New York, systematic and successful research on whether one can telepathically influence sleeping subjects has been going on for several years.

It is not odd then, and in fact it is highly consistent with the evidence, that telepathically induced UFO sightings occur when the subject is initially asleep. Berthold E. Schwarz, a New Jersey psychiatrist, reported a series of ESP-induced UFO accounts from Port Monmouth, New Jersey, which is about ten miles from New York City. In this case, ESP interrupted the sleep of a primary witness on several occasions and each time led to a UFO observation.

The case centered on Mrs. D.J., a thirty-three-year-old housewife. According to the report, she "suddenly woke up for no apparent reason and looked out her open, second-floor window." There, hovering over the meadows, she saw a glowing whitish ball which was bouncing back and forth across the field and flashing wildly. Mrs. D.J. estimated that the object was about the size of a garage. A week later, she was again suddenly awakened and tried to rouse her husband, "for I felt," she said, "that something was going to happen. It was a funny feeling—I was scared half to death." Five minutes later, a glowing ball of light fell from the sky. These experiences were followed by more UFO activity in the Port Monmouth area.

Mrs. D.J.'s experiences did not end there, for after these first UFO encounters the entire family became jinxed and all sorts of poltergeist antics broke out in their house. If UFOs are space vehicles, why should a witness find his home subsequently invaded by a poltergeist unless the UFO was in fact part of the poltergeist to begin with? In the last chapter, I showed that "miracles" and poltergeists share common ground. I think we can expand this theory to include UFOs as well. Could UFO phenomena be a poltergeist-like projection from the minds of the witnesses? The Port Monmouth incidents certainly indicate that it is possible.

UFOs: Space Vehicles or Psychic Entities? 97

The Port Monmouth visitations began in 1970 when Mrs. D.J. began awakening from sleep in time to watch glowing discs bombard the rural area around her New Jersey home. There can be little doubt that something *physical* was active in the town. UFO investigators found tripodlike marks and circular compressed areas of grass in the meadows over which the D.J. family had seen the aerial displays. According to a news story in *The Courier,* a Middleton, New Jersey-based paper, a UFO investigator, Walter Garner, discovered that even after two weeks the grass was still flattened. Garner added that the grass which was "still living would not stand erect, yet grass flattened by footsteps quickly bounced back."

Eventually the UFOs even began to center on the D.J. household. According to the testimony of Mrs. D.J.'s son Billy, an aerial disc levitated off the ground only sixty feet from the house and glided away when police investigators called at the house.

It was during this phase of the invasion that the poltergeist antics began. At first it was hard to tell whether the strange outbreak plaguing the family was psychic or merely the result of electrical disturbances. The TV set was the first appliance to function abnormally. It would continue to flicker even after all the tubes had been replaced. The ignition system of Mr. D.J.'s car suffered next. It failed five times, sometimes even when he was out driving the city streets. A mechanic was called in and replaced the system, but it continued to malfunction. Then the phone started to go haywire. Although the D.J.s had an unlisted phone number, they received two to ten phantom phone calls a day. The phone would ring, but no one would be on the line when it was answered.

So far, it is hard to judge whether or not these disturbances were electrical or psychic. But there are indications that normal explanations for the harassment will not do. Trained repairmen were at a loss to fix either the television or the car. Why? On the other hand, in some poltergeist cases, the outbreaks initially mimic electrical disturbances. A famous case in a law office in Rosenheim, Germany which was investigated by Dr. Hans Bender of Freiburg University, was at first put down to electrical dysfunction. It began as lights, electrical works, and phones began malfunctioning. Only later did it escalate. Objects were thrown and the overhead lights swung about by themselves. Another noteworthy parallel between the Rosenheim poltergeist and the Port Monmouth case was that in both outbreaks telephones were singled out for particular trouble. In the Rosenhein case, nonexistent phone calls were registered to the office phones, the call lights activated wildly, etc. So even though the Port Monmouth disturbances seem electrical, they are also very much within the repertoire of the poltergeist.

The outbreak in the D.J. home in no way lessened the activity of the UFOs which constantly invaded the area all that summer. As Mrs. D.J. recalled:

> My ten-year-old son said, "Look at the bright star." We looked up and I knew I'd seen this before. "That's no star—it's moving. It's not a plane because it stopped." We were all eyes then, as it moved across the highway. It came so close it was like a big light, but with no form behind it ... yellowish white. It seemed to follow the car. When we were halfway down the highway, it veered off to the left and went over the bay. This happened on about ten occasions ... usually on Fridays. It scared us.

It was only about two months after the initial sightings that the first genuine poltergeist activities started plaguing the D.J. family. Mrs. D.J. had just trotted up the stairs of her two-story home when:

> ... there was a smell in the bedroom: rotten like death. I never noticed this before, or since. I woke up my husband. The smell was not from the meadows. It made me want to vomit ... My husband noticed the odor also ...

Unusual odors, especially foul ones, are rather commonly reported in the poltergeist reports that have come down to us from the nineteenth century. During a wild poltergeist eruption in Tennessee during the 1810s, one of the witnesses awoke from sleep to find his bedclothes reeking with a stagnant odor. He described it as "... the most offensive stench I ever smelled."

Like many poltergeist victims, Mrs. D.J. began to suffer psychosomatic aches, sleep disturbances, pathological dreams, and similar troubles. It is not odd to find that, as a child, Mrs. D.J. had had some well-witnessed UFO encounters with her family.

Berthold Schwarz, the chief investigator of the case, was also witness to a poltergeistlike prank, so there was at least one outside witness to the disturbances. Schwarz was interviewing the family with a Sony-Auto-Sensor, thirty-minute cassette, Sony TC-100 compact set tape recorder. The re-

UFOs: Space Vehicles or Psychic Entities? 99

corder seemed to be in good working order. A few hours later, however, Schwarz discovered that key portions of the interview were missing from the tape. This had never happened before or since, and a professional repairman could not account for the mysterious erasure. It was just another enigma in the case.

It is unlikely it was by pure coincidence that the UFO visitations and the poltergeist occurrences simultaneously tormented the family. But such reports are not unique in the annals of UFO lore. There are several other cases on record in which there seems to be a direct link between a UFO encounter and a subsequent poltergeist outbreak. During the famous Yorba Linda sighting of 1967, one poltergeist made a conspicuous racket.

Yorba Linda, a sleepy little town about forty miles south of the sprawling Los Angeles megalopolis, is a middle class suburb that borders the Santa Ana Mountains. On January 24, 1967, Tom X. (as he was designated in the report) was upstairs in his parents' home getting ready to do his homework. It was raining outside, and as he glanced out a window to check the weather, he saw a peculiar top-hat shaped object hovering over the houses across the street. Tom grabbed a camera, took a snapshot of the UFO, and later turned it over to NICAP (National Investigations Committee on Aerial Phenomena) for analysis. He then ran downstairs to call his family to the window so that they could see the object for themselves, but the UFO had vanished by the time they were able to get to this vantage point. Nevertheless, Tom was able to give investigators a detailed description of the object. It was metallic but had a rather dull black surface that did not reflect light; four slender legs extended from its bottom side.

The Yorba Linda sighting was throughly investigated by NICAP in July, 1967, and analysis of the case and the photograph continued for four years. The only news release on the case appeared as a brief item in the July 7, 1967, issue of a local Santa Ana paper, *The Register*. The report was only made public in 1973 when the principal witness was twenty years old and felt that the case should be brought to the public's attention. If the case and photograph were only a teenage hoax, it seems odd that Tom X. would wish to promulgate the tale years later.

NICAP investigators soon learned that the top-hat UFO sighting was not the first the family had encountered. This again ties in perfectly with my observation that people who see one UFO will probably have additional experiences at a later time. Tom's family had a previous UFO visitation a few weeks earlier, on January 4, during which they saw a huge, silvery football-shaped UFO "hissing—like air escaping from a tire." Tom was the first to see it and rushed to his parents' bedroom to alert them. The whole family watched the mysterious craft while his father foraged for a pair of opera glasses in order to get a better look at the object. Gradually the UFO just floated eastward and out of sight. Later, nearby El Toro Marine Base was called to ascertain if any blimps had been sent up, but the base denied conducting any aerial exercises that day.

The sighting prompted Tom to take an active interest in Ufology and led him to purchase a Mark XII camera from Sears in the hopes that he could eventually photograph a UFO. This explains why a camera was so readily available when the January 24th sighting occurred. The negative of the photograph was analyzed and carefully examined on several occasions, and nothing suspicious was ever found that would indicate that it was a fake. And so ends this 1967 UFO case. However, it gradually came to light that the UFO visitations were not the only unusual encounters the family experienced. As UFO experts interviewed the family, they discovered that since December, 1966, poltergeist activity had been occurring regularly in the house. This activity continued after the UFO sightings and lasted until August, 1967, and apparently to a lesser degree after that.

The first phenomena were more ghostly than poltergeistic. Mrs. X. awoke from sleep in either November or December (she couldn't recall the precise date), thinking that someone had called her name. As her mind began to clear, she saw a filmy figure hovering between her bed and the door. Terrified, she ran through the figure toward the door to escape from the room. On looking back, the apparition had vanished. Mr. X. also woke one night thinking that Tom had called out. He told investigators that he had also heard footsteps pacing the house when he was sure no members of the household were up and around.

Neither Tom nor his sister was immune to these psychic visitations. The sister started to become anxious and suffer mysterious psychosomatic pain, whereas Tom actually saw a phantom. He had been in the downstairs bathroom when, out of the corner of his eye, he saw a male figure walk through a closed door. He watched the ghost until it vanished from his sight. Up until the time of this apparitional experience, Mr. and Mrs. X. had not told their children about the uncanny episodes that they had experienced.

In August, 1967, the X.s moved to a new home. Usually, when a family is victimized by a poltergeist, the outbreak will follow them wherever they go. The Yorba Linda case was no exception. Even in their new home, the family was disturbed by rapping sounds from the walls and windows, a plant wavered back and forth by itself, and a cat acted strangely, as though reacting to an invisible presence. Other occurrences of a psychokinetic nature continued for an unspecified period of time.

Another psychic outbreak was reported from Woodstock in 1966. This report is replete with UFO, electrical disturbances, and poltergeist encounters. The principal witnesses were disguised in the report as Mr. and Mrs. Carrier and were interviewed by Berthold Schwarz, who published the case in the *Flying Saucer Review*.

The Carriers lived off one of Woodstock's rural roads in a rented house that was surrounded by open fields interspersed with bushy outgrowths. It was in the spring of 1966 that they began noticing strange greenish lights about six feet in diameter, shining from the fields. Sometimes the objects would fly off to investigate passing automobiles, emitting whining sounds as they went. When the lights began to focus their attention on the house, the poltergeist antics began. According to Mrs. Carrier:

> One night a strange thing happened. There was a terrifically annoying sound over the driveway. It seemed about six feet above my head. I asked my husband and he didn't hear it, nor did the girl who was staying with us. It was three in the afternoon. Later that afternoon, the girl, another lady, and I were watching TV, when suddenly the sound changed, the pitch went up and down. I looked at the girl and asked, "Do you hear that, too?" "Yes," she said, "I have been hearing it since three P.M., when I was in Kingston." No one else heard it. I went all around the house checking electrical outlets, the refrigerator, putting my ears against the furniture and other things, but could find no reason for it. The sound went into a regular pattern of oscillation. Then the sound left, and from one corner of the house it went out into the open field. It was so strong that if you stood in the corner you could feel it pass through your ears. It was remarkable; I never experienced anything like it before.
>
> I put my ear to the wall facing Overlook Mountain [and

heard] funny garbled sounds like "Tweety Pie," then like a lot of sounds all in unison, like a voice. I'm positive about this. It came three feet above the ground, like mice would talk if they could jabber—but three-foot mice? It went on for more than an hour. We walked around the house and saw nothing. Finally we looked out into the field and there was the bright green light. A man we talked to about it said it was a reflection from window glass, but I went outside and it was still there. My girlfriend and I went out together and watched the light for a while. On one side of the [green] light was a red light, one eighth the size of the green light and it moved far away from it, becoming a separate light until it disappeared . . .

[At times] one heard voices like a man, thundering clumps, like someone walking. My girlfriend heard it too . . . once I fell asleep and woke up as my girlfriend screamed. There was a noise on the roof. I told my husband, but he dismissed this as too unreal. It was the first time anything like that ever happened to me. We all heard something walking on the roof, one foot after another—not like animals scrambling. It went on for a while, and I became frightened. Before I went to sleep, they tried to contact me telepathically—this never happened before! My mind blanked out. [In my mind's eye] there was a stone image of a face. It was not grotesque, but it was so scary. It was in my mind—inside my head. I said, "Go away." I screamed, "Go away." It was debilitating. Finally it went away, but the noises from the roof went on . . .

But Mrs. Carrier's distressing experiences that spring were only a prelude to what was to become a summer full of UFO sightings. Usually the orbs of light were green and were seen not only by the Carriers but by several independent witnesses as well. Strange sirenlike noises were heard from the skies, and all during the summer horror the Carriers' poltergeist kept up its racketing antics. Mrs. Carrier told investigators that objects vanished from the house, neighbors would hear footsteps around their homes, and the telephones went haywire. Finally the Carriers gave up and moved to the city.

There is little doubt in my mind that a very definite relationship existed between the UFOs and the poltergeist in all of these cases. Poltergeists generally erupt when there is a psychologically tense family situation. Could not these intense psychological frustrations also project the UFOs? Mrs. Carrier, for example, seemed to have an almost symbiotic relationship with the UFOs. Often she was the only one to hear the odd wavelike sounds; the disturbances plagued her specifi-

UFOs: Space Vehicles or Psychic Entities? 103

cally, and it was she who felt that the aliens were prying into her mind. Compare Mrs. Carrier's report to the Yorba Linda case where the UFOs appeared smack in the middle of a poltergeist outbreak, and to the D.F. family where UFOs heralded poltergeist activity in the home.

These poltergeist cases reveal a closer connection between psychic phenomena and UFO manifestations than do the telepathic cases outlined earlier. It could be argued that since ESP focuses around just about any traumatic episode—death, accident, or misfortune—some ESP cases might focus coincidentally on UFO activity. There may be no intrinsic relationship between the UFO and the subject's extrasensory awareness of it, just as there may be no relationship between an automobile accident and a subject's ESP vision of it. All that these telepathic cases *indicate* is that a special relationship exists, again perhaps a symbiotic one, between the person who sees the UFO and the UFO itself. The case, however, is not strong. But these *poltergeist* cases are a different matter entirely. We know that generally the poltergeist is projected by the minds and emotions of the household members themselves. In each of the three cases summarized above, the families were tormented by phenomena that fall right in line with the poltergeist's varied repertoire of annoying tricks. The similarities between classical poltergeist reports and these UFO incidents are too close to be happenstance. Once again, I feel that these cases indicate that, far from being space vehicles, UFOs are psychic entities created by the viewers. This is not to say that the UFOs are hallucinations. Not at all. The objects are very real but are created by some mysterious force within our own minds and bodies.*

In these cases, the UFOs were probably psychic projections, just as the poltergeist antics were. The UFOs were ac-

* There is yet another correlation between poltergeist activity and UFO sightings. In an article "Time Correlations Between Geomagnetic Disturbances and Eye-Witness Accounts of UFOs," which appeared in the July, 1974, issue of the *Flying Saucer Review*, C. Pahler has shown that there is a relationship between geomagnetic disturbances and accelerated UFO activity. W. G. Roll, of the Psysical Research Foundation in Durham, North Carolina, has pointed out that the onset of poltergeist activity also corresponds to geomagnetic disturbances. (See his "Geomagnetic Perturbation and RSPK" in *Research in Parapsychology, 1973*, Metuchen, N.J.: Scarecrow Press). It is now known that atmospheric disturbances have a profound effect on our behavior and can cause irritability and tension that might explode into poltergeist activity. The geomagnetic disturbances would be a catalyzing, not a causative factor in the outbreak.

tual elements of the potergeist. The poltergeist's nefarious activity is a way of harassing a family. What could be more provoking than a UFO?

The spontaneous healing of disease and illness has been a sign of the miraculous since time immemorial. From biblical narratives, to Lourdes, to the laying-on of hands, man has sought the miracle of healing for centuries. Recently parapsychologists in both the United States and Canada have been actively investigating healing. They have found that some gifted psychics can make seeds sprout and grow better than control seeds, that they can heal wounds on mice faster than the normal rate of healing, as well as attenuate the effects of anesthesia and affect catalysts in the body. This is a far cry from Jesus raising Lazarus from the dead, but it does show that somewhere in the human organism is a curative power that can be transferred from one individual to another.

Cases of healing are notoriously difficult to investigate. The human body is so mysterious, spontaneous remission from illness so common, and diagnosis so often faulty that it becomes nearly impossible to verify if a recovery from illness is truly miraculous. The body itself is miraculous. Certain diseases, such as cancer, do sometimes reverse their degenerative pattern. Moreover, since diagnoses often differ from one doctor to another, the difficulties inherent in studying cases of psychic healing rest not only on determining if a cure was medically improbable but on making sure that the patient actually had what he thought he had in the first place!

For example, I once thought I had developed a hernia. I had all the classic symptoms, including aches, pains, and burning sensations in the groin. I went to my doctor, and after a check-up, he confirmed my suspicions. He advised me that I might as well get prepared for surgery. I thought to myself, "Here would be a perfect test for psychic healing, since hernias don't cure themselves." I made some initial plans but never carried them through. As the burning and aching worsened, it was clear to me that the surgeon's scalpel wasn't too distant. Seeking to verify my doctor's verdict, I visited a specialist for another check-up and discovered that I had not had a hernia to begin with! Although I was, of course, relieved, I was beset by the thought, "What if I *had* gone to a healer?" The misdiagnosis would have played into the hands of the psychic, and no doubt the case would have been paraded as another well-attested "psychic healing," rather than what it was—simple medical incompetence. This illustrates only one of the problems implicit in trying to verify a case of psychic healing.

Despite these formidable problems, there are some rather sensational "cures" on record. Some of the Lourdes cases certainly command our respect. But writers and experts on healing—psychic, Christian Science, and others—often overlook one fascinating area of inquiry—those cases on record where psychic healings have occurred during UFO encounters!

By far the best-substantiated report of a UFO-induced healing is the strange case of Dr. X., which was first reported in detail by the French Ufologist Aimé Michel, who knew the percipient personally. Since Dr. X. is a prominent citizen of the French town in which he lives, his identity has been kept secret. This, however, does not detract from the case, for he was interviewed by several Ufologists who made a photographic record of some of the more bizarre aspects of the case.

At the time of his UFO encounter in 1968, Dr. X. was in anything but good health. While fighting in Algeria some years earlier he had suffered head injuries when a mine exploded. The damage to his right side had never totally healed, and up until 1968 he was often in pain. It was even impossible for him to balance himself on his right foot. To complicate matters, on October 29, 1968, Dr. X. struck himself in the leg as he was chopping wood, inflicting a wound right above the inner ankle and causing a broken vein, swelling, and acute pain. Even after two days, there was little improvement in the discomfort he was suffering.

It was on the night of November 1st that Dr. X. had his UFO experience. He was still convalescing, but despite the pain, he could not ignore the calls of his fourteen-month-old baby. He slipped painfully from bed, noticed the storm-threatening weather outside, and found his son standing erect in his cot, pointing excitedly toward the window. The shutters were closed, but Dr. X. could see flashes of light between them. Lightning, no doubt, he thought to himself. After caring for the infant, Dr. X. went back upstairs, and out of an unshuttered window noticed that the countryside was being periodically illuminated by powerful flashes.

It was while trying to determine the nature of the flashes that Dr. X. first spotted the UFO. His curiosity had been so piqued by the lights that he actually went out of the house in his pajamas and looked over the area from his hillside house.

There, to his astonishment, two identical luminous objects were hovering over the land. The craft were oval in shape, glistening silvery-white and red, and had protruding antennae on top. Each UFO emitted a shaft of white light from its underside. As Dr. X. watched, the two saucers maneuvered in parallel motions and then gradually merged together. As though by some intelligence, the now-single UFO's spotlight began to move toward Dr. X. It gradually crossed the countryside, moving toward the doctor's house, until the beam actually fell right on him. Dr. X. covered his face instinctively. A bang resounded all around him, and when he lowered his hands, he found that the ship had disappeared, leaving only a white cloud in the sky, which quickly disintegrated. From the midst of the space that had been occupied by the craft, a threadlike protuberance shot higher into the sky and disappeared with a firecracker-like sound.

The entire incident lasted only ten minutes. A very shocked Dr. X. went nervously back to his bedroom. Excited by the occurrence, he quickly woke his wife. It was at that moment that Dr. X. realized that he had not been discomforted at all by his leg which had been causing him such agony. Not only had the swelling gone down, but the wound had healed!

Dr. X. went to sleep after the incident, but that was not the end of his strange adventure. It was really only the beginning. During his subsequent slumber, Dr. X. began to talk in his sleep, mumbling that "Contact will be reestablished by falling down the stairs on November 2nd." Upon waking later that morning, he could remember *nothing* about the UFO incident. Mrs. X. even had to show him the sketches he had made of the objects right after the sighting. It was useless; Dr. X. had total amnesia about the events. Yet, just as prophesied in his sleep, Dr. X. fell down the living room stairs that afternoon (November 2nd) and suddenly recalled the night's adventure.

However, the strangest developments in the case came later that day when the doctor began to suffer from curious cramps and pains around the umbilical region. The pain did not subside for an entire week, and itching and prickly sensations irritated the area. By November 18th, a perfect geometric triangle of dark pigmentation had formed over his navel, 17 cms. by 14 to 15 cms., and all irritation stopped. Dr. X. called Aimé Michel and a dermatologist to investigate the odd skin discoloration for it was causing him acute anxiety, though no discomfort. The dermatologist could find no explanation for the mark and even wanted to report the case to the Academy of Medicine. At first, Dr. X. thought the mark might have been caused psychosomatically, since a few days earlier he had had a dream about a UFO in which the triangle symbol was conspicuous. *However, the next day the same discoloration appeared over his baby's stomach.* It was in the same area, but the triangle was formed much more crudely. After the UFO encounter, Dr. X's health began to improve, and by May, 1969, all residual pain from his war wounds had completely vanished.

This report highlights the fact that UFOs are both physical and nonphysical at the same time. The fact that two witnesses saw the UFO (if we can include the baby) and that it lit up the whole countryside certainly indicates that this UFO was a physical object. Yet its plasticity, its ability to merge with its sister craft and dematerialize, is just what one would expect from a semiphysical object. Like apparitions and hauntings, UFOs seem to travel that border between the three-dimensional and the nondimensional. As in the poltergeist-UFO reports cited earlier, there is more than casual evidence that somehow the UFO and Dr. X's mind were linked by a psychic bond. The way the object focused its attention on him, its disappearance after making contact, the doctor's amnesia yet subconscious knowledge of the incident, and the physical after-effects on his own body all lead me believe that the UFO was directly related to Dr. X. and probably caused psychically by him.

The curious marks on Dr. X's stomach and the corresponding discoloration around his baby's navel are also evidential. Is it coincidence that for ages there has been an ancient tradition that psychic force emanates from that area? Many psychics have described burning or otherwise unpleasant sensations in the pit of the stomach right before and during the production of psychic phenomena. Such sensitives as the late Eileen Garrett, the English medium Douglas Johnson, and others have all stated that the pit of the stomach is a key area in the production of the psychic force. In the Yogic tradition, this area is considered a storehouse of psychic energy and some psychics complain of physical shock to their stomachs if they are disturbed from a trance or during their psychic demonstrations. I don't think this is all coincidence. Could Dr. X. have drawn energy from himself and his infant son to create the UFO, the process of which also caused the pigmentation? Several psychic researchers of the early twentieth century noted that after psychic demonstrations, *all* those in attendance had lost small amounts of weight. Dr. W.J. Crawford, of the Queen's University of Belfast, carried out extensive tests with a nineteen-year-old medium, Kathleen Goligher, who could levitate tables. After every sitting, *all* the sitters had lost small amounts of weight, as though power had been taken from them.

This "withdrawal of power" may also explain why cars malfunction during UFO encounters. Could it be that here, too, the human agent draws energy not only from himself but from any readily available energy source? In poltergeist cases, for instance, electrical disturbances are frequent. It is hard to believe that the human body has an inherent force capable of moving extremely heavy objects. Instead, some poltergeist experts, such as Dr. Hans Bender, believe that the agent withdraws energy from the atmosphere and other sources as well and then redirects it. If this theory is correct and we can create UFOs through our psychic potential, one might find that the force needed to create the manifestation has been withdrawn from nearby power sources and then redirected. Cars would stall, lights would go out or flicker, appliances would malfunction, etc., just as has been actually reported during UFO appearances.

If Dr. X.'s case were unique, we could brush it under the carpet as an anomaly. As everyone knows, science has a rather nasty habit of ignoring facts that run counter to generally accepted theories. But Dr. X.'s report is *not* unique. There are many other cases on record which report that UFO percipients have found themselves healed of all sorts of complaints. While most of them lack the strong evidence of the case of Dr. X., the sheer volume of these UFO-related healings form a striking pattern. The British Ufologist Gordon Creighton has made a chronological study of several modern cases which he reported in the September–October, 1969, issue of the *Flying Saucer Review*. In many cases, the healings seem to be linked to a mysterious light that was projected from the UFOs. Here are two of the reports:

On the night of September 3, 1965, Chief Deputy Billy McCoy and Patrol Deputy Robert Goode of Brazona County, Texas, were driving along a highway south of Damon. Deputy Goode was suffering a great deal of pain from a bite on his finger inflicted by his pet alligator. The finger had bled and become swollen. Goode could think of nothing but the

UFOs: Space Vehicles or Psychic Entities? 109

pain. Their drive was going along uneventfully until midnight when a gigantic UFO suddenly illuminated the sky. McCoy and Goode estimated the flying saucer to be 200 feet long and 50 feet thick. According to the officers' report, both men became terrified and tried to speed off, but the UFO shot a brilliant light into their car which fell right on Goode's left hand and arm. When the officers had calmed down after this breathtaking ordeal, Goode realized that the pain and swelling were gone and unusually rapid healing of the wound followed.

A very similar healing was recorded in Peru. On December 9, 1968, a customs official claimed that he had seen a flying saucer from the terrace of his house. It emitted violent rays that projected over his face. The official was myopic and had to wear thick glasses, but after the encounter he found that both his myopia and rheumatism had been cured. The case was investigated by Peruvian APRO (Aerial Phenomena Research Organization) representatives.

There are definite parallels between these cases. The appearance of the projected light beams, the nocturnal nature of the UFOs, and the unusually rapid healing all follow a consistent pattern. There is an even more remarkable parallel between the cases of Dr. X. and Deputy Goode. In both cases, the UFOs were seen shortly after the witnesses had suffered painful injuries; they were almost instantaneously immunized against the pain, and rapid healing of their physical wounds followed. Is this coincidence or did the UFOs come (or materialize) in answer to an unconscious though urgent need?

There is also a symbolic element in these healings. As I said earlier, healing has always been a sign of the miraculous. There were many miraculous healings reported at Fatima and Zeitoun. The instantaneous deliverance from pain and longstanding suffering reported during these religious outbreaks directly parallel the UFO healings we have cited. Parapsychology has now proved that man has a healing potential hidden within his own organism. If he can create the miraculous by materializing UFO visitors, could he not create these vehicles with healing powers as well? Surely this theory is no more bizarre than believing that UFOs are spacecraft from distant planets and galaxies.

So far, I have not commented on "occupant cases," which are reports in which the primary witness either sees or interacts with beings who emerge from or are seen around UFOs. To many people these cases are perhaps the most credulity-stretching of all, even though there is no rational reason why they should be met with any greater skepticism than any other type of UFO report. For some emotional or psychological reason, people who might be willing to believe that UFOs are trafficking our skies are extremely reluctant to admit any sort of direct human contact with alien beings. Yet occupant cases are reported fairly regularly.

Perhaps the most classic occupant report, and for our purposes the most illustrative, is the April 24, 1964, Socorro, New Mexico, case, which has become a standard warhorse in the Ufology repertoire. On the afternoon of April 24th, policeman Lonnie Zamora was on duty and at 5:45 P.M. was pursuing a speeding car south of town. Although there had been recent reports of UFO activity in the area, Zamora never had any personal encounter. But as he was making his high-speed chase his attention was suddenly distracted by a flame-emitting UFO which was flying overhead. He was so distracted, in fact, that he gave up his pursuit. However, Zamora was able to spy on the craft after it landed, and he saw two white-cloaked figures bustling about close to the ship. Zamora drove around a hill that partially obscured his view, and he perched himself at a higher elevation. Looking down from there into a gully, he saw what he later described as an egg-shaped metallic UFO resting on supporting legs. He was less than 150 feet from the object when the craft began to emit loud noises. Zamora ran for shelter, and by the time he was able to look back over his shoulder, the craft had taken off and shot up into the air. All that was left at the landing site were some pole marks and burned greasewood plants. Zamora had radioed in his report right after he spotted the UFO, but by the time a fellow officer arrived on the scene, the UFO was gone. However, the plants were still smoldering.

These occupant cases would seem to refute any theory that UFOs and UFO-allied phenomena are psychic projections. Lights in the sky, perhaps, but landed spaceships complete with pilots and navigators, hardly! These reports could serve as strong evidence that UFOs are exactly what they seem to be—spacecraft piloted from other worlds. But in looking over these occupant cases, one soon realizes that *on some occasions the witnesses were vaguely aware that the entities they saw were partially nonphysical.* In one recorded case, some

UFOs: Space Vehicles or Psychic Entities?

teen-agers chased a group of silver-suited UFO-nauts across a muddy field. Yet the beings left no tracks. In other cases, witnesses noted that the beings were semitransparent. So the UFO occupants may actually be no more real than apparitions. One Ufologist, Luis Schönherr has written:

> Loosely speaking the entities seen in connection with UFOs seem to have difficulties with their extremities. Witnesses report that they could see no arms, or that they had the impression that they were held close to the body.
>
> In one case the witness noted quite definitely that the legs of the entities were transparent—he could see the grass through them. Others reported that the lower part of the body seemed "indistinct," or hidden by high grass. Phenomenologically both statements could refer to the same category of phenomenon. Whether someone says the legs were transparent, or that the grass was visible through them, or whether another person says the legs were hidden by the grass, they amount to basically the same thing.

Schönherr goes on to point out the similarities between these UFO-nauts and the appearance of conventional apparitions. In apparitional cases, the entire figure does not usually appear. Instead, witnesses often state that the phantoms only appeared from the bust up. This is the portion of the body by which we recognize one another or foreign people. Schönherr goes on to shrewdly point out:

> It is a fact that people usually have the most precise memory of the physiognomy, the head and upper part of a person's body, while the colour of the shoes, for example, is often not only forgotten, but possibly not even perceived.
>
> It seems not unreasonable to assume that the same mental process may play a role in the generation of hallucinatory experiences, whether they be séance-room materializations or UFO entities.
>
> One could even argue that the internal mechanics and logic of the process of hallucinatory perception would demand that for images that cannot be experienced within the framework of a hallucination (because there may be no pertaining information in the memory-strata accessible in such a case), other images are sometimes substituted in order to maintain logic and consistency of the experience.
>
> Seen from this angle, the missing-leg pattern would possibly have to be suspected in other disguises, as for example in those sightings where UFO-entities have been reported wearing monklike cowls or gowns, or have been seen within

UFOs with their legs partially concealed by the object's structure.

The latter would mean that not only the entities but also the objects—or whatever the observer perceives of them—are hallucinatory experiences.

It has often been argued that the sort of experiences reported by witnesses of UFO-landings and of entities cannot be hallucinations because such extensive and consistent hallucinations are only known to occur in pronounced pathological subjects—a category of percipients to which the majority of UFO witnesses definitely do not belong.

This argument, however, does not take into account the possibility that conditions may exist in the vicinity of a UFO which stimulate hallucinatory experiences even in mentally sound and perfectly normal people which are comparable in quality and degree to the pathological cases.

In the field of UFOs, as well as in parapsychology, there are other things, however, that do not fit into the hallucination hypothesis. . . .

When facts do not fit the theory, either one or the other has to be thrown out. In conventional science it is usually the facts that are the first to go! Schönherr has made some strong points. But because a sighting is a likely psychic projection, does this projection have to be totally subjective? As the Fatima and Welsh revival miracles indicate, psychic projections can be physically very real. Apparitions, for example, often take on physical attributes. While they do have the nasty habit of walking through walls and appear dressed in ethereal clothing, they also have the propensity to move objects and are often collectively seen. Apparitions represent an interface between mind and matter. They are partly physical, yet partly mental. UFOs and UFO occupants might fall into a similar pattern—projections from our own minds that take on the characteristics and the ability to manipulate real matter. They might be "real" in every sense of the word, but still be products of our own psychic potential.

The UFO-psychic projection theory gains more support when we take into consideration the fact that some psychics have the ability to create UFOs habitually. Earlier I pointed out that Ivan Sanderson's unusually frequent encounters with mysterious aerial objects were telltale indications that he was creating them himself. In the previous chapter I showed that the aerial lights seen during the Welsh revival focused on and followed Mrs. Mary Jones, who was also in all probability actually creating them. It seems plausible that many mod-

UFOs: Space Vehicles or Psychic Entities? 113

ern "contactees" (those people who think they are in communication with alien entities) are really involved in a gigantic psychic charade. They have psychically created the UFOs and their occupants, who have taken on lives and intelligences of their own. It is rather like an objectified daydream. Most contactee stories are blatantly absurd, others are downright hoaxes. Even the famous "contactee" George Adamski, who was a pioneer figure in the saucer craze, admitted to a friend of mine that he had taken up "this saucer business" because the end of prohibition had put a stop to the profit from his religious cult. The cult had made religious (and opportune) use of alcohol legally and Adamski had cashed in on the profit!

Other contactees seem sincere, even though their stories are no less ridiculous than the hoaxers. One man might claim in all sincerity that he has flown in a flying saucer, while another contactee may swear that UFO-nauts visit him nightly in his home. There is a possibility that these cases are neither hoaxes nor true delusions but psychic realities. Perhaps we can call it a form of psychic paranoia. Yet some of the contactees have been able to share their experiences with outside witnesses. One psychic who believes herself to be in contact with UFO entities is Stella Lansing, a Massachusetts housewife. She had reported a bizarre history of UFO sightings and encounters, and outside witnesses have accompanied her on her UFO hunts. There can be little doubt that she is psychic. Her whole life story is highlighted by reports of telepathy, precognition, psychokinesis, etc., and there can be no doubt that these faculties have an obvious bearing on her UFO experiences.

The case of Stella Lansing came to the attention of Dr. Berthold Schwarz during an APRO symposium in Maryland in January, 1971. Schwarz was the perfect investigator to handle the case, since in addition to being a psychiatrist he has a strong background in parapsychology and Ufology. After his talk he had planned on lunching with J. Allen Hynek but was persuaded by a friend to attend a talk given by Mrs. Lansing. As Schwarz reminisced:

> I spent the time in the auditorium listening to one of the most unusual accounts of alleged repeated close UFO contacts that I have ever heard. On the surface the data were extraordinary if not preposterous: experiences involving strange little men, voices appearing out of nowhere, creatures, loss of consciousness, "electric shock" from a shimmer-

ing figure, a gaping round hole in the ice, a craft possibly surfacing from under water, minuscule footprints, religious symbols, bizarre harassments, etc....

But since Mrs. Lansing had kept detailed records of all her experiences, Schwarz was reluctant to dismiss the case out-of-hand. If nothing else, the case might at least be a psychiatrist's dream. Schwarz began analyzing the case, which at first didn't seem too promising. After all, Mrs. Lansing did have a history of mental illness, and her UFO stories seemed more pathological than parapsychological. Just after her first UFO encounter in 1967, she became acutely unbalanced. No one would listen to her stories with an open mind, and her Catholic upbringing led her to believe that the experiences were evil. Ultimately, Mrs. Lansing had to be hospitalized for paranoid schizophrenia on two occasions. Following her second hospital stay, which lasted five weeks, she has had no recurrence of her psychotic symptoms. Of course, the question remains: Did the mental illness give rise to the UFOs, or did the UFOs give rise to the mental illness?

But even after her release, her UFO sightings and contacts persisted and gradually caused psychic manifestations. She would receive ESP impressions as to when and where the UFOs would appear and even had a veridical dream about what the UFO-nauts would look like. Had it not been for the presence of outside witnesses to some of these experiences it would be easy to dismiss her reports as merely the rantings of a disturbed woman.

In February, 1971, Schwarz himself accompanied Mrs. Lansing on a UFO field trip. He wasn't disappointed:

> ... After an evening of intensive interviewing of Mrs. Lansing and her lady and gentleman friends, I went with her, at 4:00 A.M. to one of her favorite UFO sites, overlooking a hilltop that was cleared for high-tension wires. At that time the dark sky was suddenly lit up and we saw a round, pulsating, bright yellow-orange, noiselessly gliding light, which expanded and contracted, went out and relighted. Mrs. Lansing intermittently photographed this over several minutes, while I tape-recorded the event. Stars and the moon were also seen and photographed as controls ...

Schwarz made a second field exploration with Stella Lansing on April 15, accompanied by a middle-aged lady friend of the psychic. At 10:45 P.M. the trio arrived at a rural New England site and within minutes,

> ... the sky over the nearby hill across the field was illuminated by a sudden appearance of one, and then two, white-yellowish-orange discs, which pulsated, changed size and color, and merged into one, and then separated into two discs; then they noiselessly glided away at varying speeds.

Schwarz tried to make a tape recording of the event, but his Sony cassette recorder refused to function.

A third trip was made, but both Mrs. Lansing and Schwarz had the intuitive feeling that nothing would happen. The night was a total blank.

Schwarz is not the only investigator to witness Mrs. Lansing's UFO encounters. When British Ufologist I. Gratton-Guinness visited with Schwarz and Mrs. Lansing at the psychiatrist's New Jersey home, the evening was highlighted by an almost typical UFO sighting. As the English investigator reported:

> A light, which we had already filmed as a star, suddenly moved silently and rapidly in a shallowly descending path behind Dr. Schwarz's house. Unfortunately, we have no record of the sighting, for Mrs. Lansing had no premonition of its occurrence. But we both reacted simultaneously and spontaneously to it, and described it in exactly the same detail afterwards. Although the motion was rapid, it was slow enough for me to notice its slightly oscillatory character. It was nothing like the motion of a meteor or a falling star, for the object neither left trail nor followed a conical path.

During the course of her experiences and experiments, Mrs. Lansing has often photographed UFOs. Many of the photographs show clusters of them posed in curious clock-face-like formations. If one analyzes the scale, the optics, and other photographic features, it is hard to believe that Mrs. Lansing was actually photographing objects in the sky. Two alternate explanations for these photographs can be advanced. Either Mrs. Lansing faked them or she had psychokinetically imprinted the UFO images directly onto the film.

Today psychic photography is a topic not held in very high regard within the field of parapsychology. In the early years of psychical research there were many investigations of psychics who claimed that they could impress their thoughts onto photographic plates. But photographic hanky-panky was so easy to accomplish that in retrospect most of these reports are not as impressive today as they were fifty years ago. Nonetheless some *are* still impressive when read today. Professor T. Fukurai of the University of Tokyo wrote a book on his own experiments, *Clairvoyance and Thoughtography* (London: Rider, 1931), in which he reported that he had found several subjects who could impress Japanese characters, faces, or pictures onto sealed photographic plates under test conditions. The phenomenon of thought-photography had a resurgence in the 1960s when news stories about a Chicago bellhop named Ted Serios started to hit the psychic press. According to the reports, Serios could stare into a Polaroid camera and impress pictures onto the film. Curtis Fuller, the publisher of *Fate* magazine, brought the reports to the attention of Dr. Jule Eisenbud, a Denver-based psychoanalyst, who took Serios under his wing. During extensive tests, Eisenbud demonstrated that Ted could impress images onto film even through lead-shielded glass and could psychially imprint on a snapshot an image which matched a picture that had remained hidden from his physical view in a sealed envelope. On one occasion, Serios also impressed an image on several frames of motion picture film. After many months of ingenious tests, Serios seemed to lose his ability and now leads a very quiet life back in Chicago.

Stella Lansing's UFO pictures could very well have been psychic projections on film. In one article about the photographs, Schwarz reported that Mrs. Lansing was able to superimpose humanlike figures and odd configurations on snapshots taken out of doors and indoors. In all probability these were psychic influences on the film comparable to the ones Serios was able to produce. It also seems apparent that Mrs. Lansing has the requisite psychokinetic ability needed to obtain thought photographs. On one occasion when Mrs. Lansing and the Schwarzes were visiting, a wall tile was mysteriously detached from its position, and a cup and saucer fell from a kitchen counter. This had never happened before, and Schwarz was sure that it was due to Mrs. Lansing's psychokinesis.

What are we to make of all this? I fail to see much evidence that Mrs. Lansing is in contact with alien beings. But one cannot dismiss the fact that the UFOs she sees are obviously real and that she is somehow linked to them. Her premonitions about when and where they will appear, their visual appearance in her presence, and her bizarre encounters

UFOs: Space Vehicles or Psychic Entities?

all prove that there is a connection between her mind and the UFO phenomena. It is also quite clear that Mrs. Lansing is psychic, and her earlier personal history leads me to believe that she might be suffering from a severe mental disturbance as well. The delusion that one's mind is being invaded by alien thoughts or being pried into, or that one is in contact with otherworld intelligences is not an infrequent delusion among paranoids and paranoid-schizophrenics. Could Mrs. Lansing be suffering from paranoid delusions which she has built up into an elaborate UFO fantasy? And then could it be possible that she has used her psychic abilities and powers to reinforce, *objectify*, and materialize her delusions? This explanation would fit the facts. This whole psychic charade could serve as a safety-valve to keep her from a total psychotic breakdown.

Sometimes a very fine line exists between the psychic, the psychotic, and the psychopath. As I began to investigate psychic after psychic, I soon realized that many out-and-out grifters originally may have had a slight degree of ability. Not much, mind you, but something. It was usually the fruitless attempts by these self-proclaimed miracle-workers to commercialize their fleeting abilities that led them into fraud. If some UFO contactees combine a psychological mixture of the paranoid and the pathologic with psychic aptitudes, we might find some glimmer of truth behind their exaggerated claims.*

The fact that a UFO percipient can use his psychic potential to objectify or reinforce his delusions can also explain some of the oddities that crop up in Ufology all the time. It sheds new light, for example, on such mysteries as Trevor James and his photographs of the UFO-like space animals which he has affectionately called "the critters." Let's take a look at this puzzle.

At the beginning of this chapter it was pointed out that many experts believe that UFOs are really space animals that feed on energy. The Viennese patron of psychic studies, Zoe Wassilko-Serecki, first proposed this theory, and such Ufolo-

---

* Any discussion on the psychic aspect of UFO contactees should include the Israeli psychic Uri Geller. However, so much has been written about this provocative psychic that I shall refrain from repeating it all here. However, I have analyzed Geller and his mentor Dr. Andrija Puharich and their claims of extraterrestrial contact elsewhere and find no evidence to support their rather wild stories. This critique is given in my contribution, "Dr. Puharich's UFO Fantasies," in Martin Ebon's anthology, *The Amazing Uri Geller* (New York: Signet Books, 1975).

gists as Ivan Sanderson, Vincent Gaddis, and John Cage have seriously considered the possibility. No one had evidence of any such ultraterrestrial beings until Trevor James came along with his unusual book, *They Live in the Sky*, in 1958.

James is actually the pseudonym for Trevor James Constable, a Los Angeles businessman and ex-New Zealand radio operator, who now lives in San Pedro, California, where he is engaged in private research. James became interested in Ufology in the 1940s and noted that a majority of sightings were coming from desert regions. It was his theory that UFOs might be animal forms which sought out those regions to escape the hustle and bustle of the cities. So he and his coworker, James O. Woods, set up field trips into the desert to photograph the skies, hoping to catch the space animals on film. At first they used an infrared telescope, hoping that its sensivity would enable them to see the creatures. When that project failed, they turned to making high-speed infrared photographs of the sky. The plan worked. Although at first they could never tell when they would catch one of the "critters" on film, James developed a psychic sensitivity to the creatures. He intuitively felt when they were overhead. As he stated in his book, "First one becomes conscious that such things exist, and then an awareness of their actual presence follows."

James' best pictures were taken right after dawn. Eventually he procured some thirty photographs showing huge, amorphous amoeba-like objects. Some of the "critters" did resemble UFO shapes. Cigar-shaped and disc-like creatures cropped up frequently on the photographs. They appear transparent, as though only two-dimensional.

Analyzing James' pictures today, over fifteen years after they were originally taken, one wonders whether the "critters" were animal beings or merely creations of his mind. James adamantly believes the former theory and had tried to collect evidence that other people have also encountered them. In 1925, long before the UFO craze, an adventurer named Don Wood claimed to have run right into one of them although his account was not published until 1959 (*Flying Saucer*, October issue). Wood and some friends were flying an old World War I vintage "Jenny" over the Nevada desert. They had landed the craft and were exploring the region on foot when they saw a saucer-shaped object coming in for a landing. Wood went on to report that "... we walked up to the thing and it was some *animal* like we never saw be-

UFOs: Space Vehicles or Psychic Entities? 119

fore. It was hurt, and as it breathed, the top would rise and fall, making a half-foot hole all around it like a clam opening and closing." As they watched, the object grew brighter and another "critter" landed atop it. Both rose into the air and shot away.

Unfortunately, when Wood's account was published in 1959, there was no statement from the other three alleged witnesses. It is also suspicious that the report was not printed until *after* the appearance of James' book. So the story must remain simply a story and nothing more. Despite James' search for evidence, there is very little independent corroboration for his beloved "critters."

Like so many other UFO percipients, James had a mental link to the objects. He *knew* when they were present and he *knew* when to photograph them. It is just as likely that he also created them. It could be that he actually projected them psychically into the sky, but that his psychic creations were too ethereal to be seen by the human eye although substantial enough to be photographed. Or, if we take into account the evidence for psychic photography, perhaps James influenced his own photos by projecting images onto the film just as Ted Serios could do. Whatever the case may be, Trevor James' *They Live in the Sky* may well be telling us more about the human mind than about the UFO mystery.

The UFO puzzle is vastly more complicated than the first Ufologists ever dreamed. At first, they tried to discern what the physical properties of these vehicles were and what means of propulsion they used. Now we are faced not only with these problems, but with even thornier questions. What are the psychic attributes of the UFOs? What is the relationship between the object seen and the viewers who see it?

As I indicated when I opened this chapter, most UFO theorists make the error of trying to find a unified explanation for all UFOs. But why? There might be many strange things in the sky: physical objects, psychic objects, interdimensional objects, *ad infinitum*. The inhabitants of the sky may be as diversified as the life forms that live in our seas.

The explanations and thoughts I have given here are only one way of looking at the UFO enigma. This is not to say that a psychic theory for this mystery is totally correct. I doubt if any theory is *totally* correct. But one thing is certain—UFOs are either the product or initiators of psychic disturbances. They are neither purely physical nor purely mental. They travel an interface between the two.

Man's mind has given birth to many miracles. The genius that went into advancing our modern technology and present science is staggering in itself. Who is to say that mind and matter are two divorced entities? The mind can create thoughts and emotions. We cannot say that our thoughts are totally personal or subjective because we know from the study of ESP that they can affect other minds as well. We also know through the study of psychokinesis that our thoughts can influence matter. And if our minds can move matter, perhaps they can create it from energy as well. When we understand the almost infinite complexities of the human mind, then and only then will we be able to fathom the mystery of the UFOs.

POSTSCRIPT

This chapter was written during the month of January, 1976. It was also during this month that I was intensively rereading and examining the entire UFO question. The theory that it is our own minds that create UFO phenomena was written in final form, revised, and corrected on January 20 and 21. The exact time of the completion of the manuscript was 4:30 P.M. January 21.

Basing my views on the encounters described by Sanderson, Keel, and others, it was my personal theory that sometime during the process of writing this chapter I would either have or participate in some form of UFO encounter. My preoccupation with UFOs and my theory about them led me to believe that it would be highly likely that I would myself become responsible for the manifestation of a UFO. This feeling became more and more intense during the period January 19–21 as my studies were nearing completion.

At 8:30 P.M. on January 21, only four hours after the final completion of this chapter and as I was casually finishing dinner in a Los Angeles restaurant, my tenant Gary W. Humecke was driving through the Malibu Hills just outside Los Angeles. Mr. Humecke did not know that I was working on a book on UFO phenomena nor about my psychic origination theory to account for them. Yet as he drove through the area, he was startled to see hovering over a gully below a huge object which he described as larger than any helicopter or plane. Although it was dark, the object had four lights on

UFOs: Space Vehicles or Psychic Entities?

top of its structure and a matching set on its underside. The lights illuninated the vehicle enough for Mr. Humecke to see that it was oval in shape. Along its center the vehicle had a series of red lights which flashed nonsequentially. The sight so startled Mr. Humecke that he stopped and left his truck to watch the strange lights.

After hovering for several seconds, the vehicle *slowly* rose at a 45 degree angle. *It emitted no sound.* After flying across a road which runs through the gully, it hovered again before slowly gliding over the hills bordering the gully and disappeared from view.

At approximately 9:30 that evening Mr. Humecke reported his experience to me. His exact words when I greeted him were, "I think I saw a UFO this evening."

The odd hovering and soundless gliding motion of the object would seem to rule out conventional aircraft.* These motions and the nonsequential lights are typically UFO-ish. However, the most intriguing aspect of the sightings is its parallel to my own work, theories, and conviction that somehow I would be engaged in a UFO experience. In fact, on the evening of January 20, I even thought to myself, "If I saw a UFO now, that would clinch my theory." As I stated earlier, UFOs do seem to show some awareness of their viewers' activities or thoughts. Again I ask the reader, What is the likelihood of a UFO appearing (1) to my tenant and friend, (2) just on the same day I completed a thorough reevaluation of the UFO mystery, and (3) just after I reached the conclusion that theoretically I should be involved somehow in a UFO incident. I should add that Mr. Humecke has no history of psychic experiences and this was his first UFO encounter. What is even more provocative is that as of this date Mr. Humecke is the only personal friend of mine to have had a conventional UFO encounter.

This strange affair is not coincidental. It is my interpretation that my involvement with UFO studies ignited a sequence of psychic activity which culminated in Mr. Humecke's sighting on the very day my own work was concluded.

---

* Needless to say, the local Air Force base reported no aerial exercises that night. Nor were they aware of any conventional aircraft that would fit Mr. Humecke's description. The Malibu sheriff's station did not receive any independent UFO reports. They too were not aware of any air activity in the Malibu area which could have been misinterpreted.

CHAPTER 5

Pascagoula Revisited: The Psychic Story

Even more bizarre than UFO occupant or contactee reports are those rare birds Ufologists call "abduction" cases. While we may snicker at the stories of those self-avowed space prophets who claim to have flown in flying saucers over the earth or to distant planets, there is a disturbing firsthand log of reports by people who claim to have been temporarily abducted by UFOs. The most famous case is that of Betty and Barney Hill, who, after driving late at night through New England's White Mountains in 1961, could not account for a mysterious time-loss of several hours. They seemed to be suffering from temporary amnesia. After months and months of anxiety and nightmares, the Hills sought psychiatric help from a prominent Boston psychiatrist-neurologist, Dr. Benjamin Simon. Simon probed into the couples' lost memories by means of hypnotic regression. Both Barney and Betty independently gave identical stories about being abducted and examined aboard a UFO. Betty even drew a replica of a star map she thought she had seen aboard the craft, and years later her diagram was matched to an actual star configuration which would be seen if one were travelling toward our solar system from the constellation Reticulum.

The Hill case, though, is not strong. There was a lapse of several months between the experience and the hypnotic regression probes. What conversations went on between them during that time? What cues, talking in their sleep, or silent understanding could they have given one another about that night during those thirty-six months? As for the map, discovering the physical existence of the stars drawn by Betty Hill was the painstaking project of Mrs. Marjorie Fish, an elementary schoolteacher from Oak Harbor, Ohio. Mrs. Fish

Pascagoula Revisited: The Psychic Story

mapped out all the stars within sixty light-years of the earth, and it was only after six months of hard work that she was able to make a match. This sounds a little too much like the "crumpled paper" effect. If you crumple up paper, coincidental patterns are sure to arise. I am sure that no matter *what* diagram Mrs. Hill had made, it would match some sort of star sequence somewhere in the universe.

One is also struck by the symbolism that permeates the Hills' case. Betty and Barney Hill had a racially mixed marriage. Betty was from a staunchly conservative white New England family, and Barney was black. They were married during a time when racial equality and acceptance was a dream, not a reality. The psychological frustration and self-questioning they must have gone through are aptly presented in their abduction tale. Hostile authoritarian figures abduct the couple, separate them, and (according to Betty Hill's hypnotic testimony) test her for pregnancy. Could these not have been the projections of very real fears about their interracial role in society and the attitude of their peers, the fears they harbored against the establishment? Is it also by coincidence that their abduction was in 1961, one of the first years of the civil rights movement when racial strife was beginning to peak?

Is Betty and Barney Hill's "interrupted journey" a case of UFO abduction or a shared paranoid fantasy which turned into a nightmare?

Amnesia is a common reaction to a UFO encounter. Not only did the Hills suffer from it, but Dr. X., whom we spoke about in the last chapter, also had no memory of his UFO experience and healing upon awakening later that morning. Usually hypnosis has been used to bring back these memories.

Besides the Hills' adventure, perhaps the most famous abduction case in which hypnosis was used is one that concerned Officer Herb Schirmer of Ashland, Nebraska. It is noteworthy because it was a sensational case based on *absolutely no evidence!* An examination of the Schirmer case reveals just how tricky hypnotic probing can be.

While driving about on December 3, Herb Schirmer saw a UFO-like object on the road ahead of him. To get a better look at the vehicle, he flashed on his high beams which seemed to provoke the UFO into a rapid takeoff. Driving back to his station, Schirmer recorded, "Saw a flying saucer at the junction of highways 6 and 63. Believe it or not." But after this incident, Schirmer began to be plagued by several symptoms as a result of his experience: headaches, buzzing sounds, insomnia, and a welt which formed below his left ear. In order to explore these symptoms, Schirmer underwent hypnotic probing, and it soon became clear that the patrolman had no recollection about a key twenty minutes during his UFO experience. Further hypnotic probing elicited a most unusual story.

It seemed that after his initial sighting, the patrolman tried to follow the UFO by car. As in so many cases, his automobile engine and radio went dead. As the UFO landed, Schirmer found himself prevented from escaping by a telepathic command. Occupants emerged from the saucer, shot some green gas toward his car, flashed a light on him, and the officer passed out. When he came to, the Ufo-nauts were talking to him. They asked about our power system, then took him aboard the spacecraft where they informed him that they had come from another galaxy and were gradually revealing themselves to mankind. They added that only bits and pieces were being revealed at first in order to puzzle man, and they told Schirmer that they had bases underwater, on Venus, under the poles, and were here on friendly business.

And so ends the case of Patrolman Schirmer.

While the case is certainly intriguing, it takes only sophomoric understanding of hypnosis and psychology to realize what really happened. There were no other witnesses to Schirmer's abduction experience, so it lacks any corroborative evidence, and both the amnesia and his story have perfectly normal explanations. In the first chapter, I spoke about "fugue states," a form of temporary amnesia used by a person to block a traumatic experience or an unmanageable life situation. For example, in their chapter, "Neurotic Behavior" in the Perry London and David Rosenhan text, *Foundations of Abnormal Psychology*, Douglas Nike and Norman Tiber write: "In *fugue states*, the person suddenly leaves his usual environment and loses all sense of identity. As in amnesia, the patient cannot recall the events which occurred during the fugue period. Usually the reaction is limited to a few hours or days." As for amnesia, Nike and Tiber wrote, "... Traumatic experiences frequently stimulate these reactions, and events before or after traumatic experiences may be forgotten."

There can be little doubt that most people would find a UFO encounter disturbing if not downright traumatic! So there is really nothing too mysterious about the fact that the Hills, Dr. X., and Patrolman Schirmer all suffered temporary bouts of amnesia. The amnesia was self-induced to escape psychologically from the memory of the ordeal.

Officer Schirmer's abduction story can be disposed of very easily as well. Hypnotic probing can produce very bizarre results, as any medically and psychologically oriented hypnotist will tell you. You can create secondary personalities, convince them that they are obsessing spirits, prod a subject into recalling a fanciful and nonexistent past life, etc. The main problem a hypnotist has to worry about is "demand characteristics," the tendency for hypnotized subjects to give responses that conform to what the hypnotist *wants or expects* to hear and receive. A good example of a demand characteristic turned up by design in an experiment carried out by hypnosis expert, M. T. Orne. He told a group of subjects that hand contraction was a normal consequence of hypnotic trance. After hypnotizing the volunteers, a majority did have hand contractions, even though that response is *not* a typical hypnotic reaction at all! In other words, the subjects responded in the way the hypnotist led them to believe they would.

A similar demand characteristic probably prompted Schirmer's account and others like it. During the process of hypnosis and re-hypnosis, Schirmer could certainly have discerned what his clinicians were looking for, so the unconscious Schirmer was apt to be more than accommodating. His story is really nothing more than a hodge-podge of pop-UFO lore, perhaps a bit of past reading, and a lot of nonsense. Even Jacques Vallee, who apparently takes the story seriously, described the UFO revelations as "possibly misleading information." Quite a euphemism, to say the least. Schirmer's story is merely a rather eclectic composition of popular UFO lore. That the space visitors are here to help us is a plot line that goes back to George Adamski and his publicized contactee con-game. The bit about bases on Venus (also an Adamski adaptation), underwater, and under the poles are all old UFO tales which go back further than Schirmer's experiences. There is a truism in the revelations in which the entities told Schirmer that they are trying to "puzzle" the human race with bits and pieces of mismatched information. Schirmer's own hypnotized mind was telling the experimenters exactly what the story really was—an incomplete jigsaw puzzle composed of the contradictory UFO lore that he had picked up over the years, and nothing more. Schirmer's mind was "puzzling" his clinicians.

I do not mean to imply that Officer Schirmer was in any way responsible for the story or fabricated it. The truly guilty parties were the hypnotists who, in their zeal, pushed the patrolman until in self-defense, his mind came up with an abduction story to placate his hypnotic tormenters.*

Actually, it wouldn't be hard to dismiss this whole abduction business if it were not for the strange events of October 11, 1973, that catapulted Pascagoula, Mississippi, into the public's eye when two otherwise normal, hard-working citizens claimed to have been abducted by a UFO. The story of Charles Hickson and Calvin Parker is already a classic UFO report that has rivaled the Hill case in evidence and melodrama. But here I would like to tell a different version of the Hickson-Parker story—a psychic story—which is being overlooked by the many Ufologists who are investigating the case. I can offer no solution to the Pascagoula case, only suggestions. So before I get to the psychic aspects of the case, let's take a brief look at this now-famous story.

Pascagoula was rife with UFO activity in October, 1973. On the night of October 11, Larry Booth, a service station operator; R. H. Broadus, a probation officer; and E. P. Sigalas, a city councilman, all saw UFOs. Sigalas stated that at first he thought what he saw while driving was a helicopter, but when he got a better view of it he saw that it was cylindrical in shape. Jim Flynt, foreman of Pascagoula's Walker Shipyard, had seen some odd aerial acrobatics as well. Booth had seen a UFO from his house. He looked out the window to see a huge multi-lighted space vehicle floating in the sky. That night, forty-four-year-old Charlie Hickson and nineteen-year-old Calvin Parker, completely oblivious to all these other sightings, were out for a late-night fishing expedition. At Hickson's suggestion, the two were fishing off a pier at Shaupeter Shipyard. The pier jutted out a few feet from the rather deserted and rubbish-littered area. Several yards to the left of the pier is a bridge which spans the Pascagoula River, ending its bypass near some ship docks on the other side. While fishing, their attention was suddenly drawn to an odd buzzing sound in the air. Looking around, they spotted a pulsating light which grew closer and closer and

* Transcripts of the actual Schirmer sessions are included in Ralph and Judy Blum's excellent book, *Beyond Earth: Man's Contact with UFOs*.

gradually took on the shape of a UFO. Hickson and Parker were nearly paralyzed with fright when they saw a door open in the vehicle, and three silvery robotlike beings "floated" toward them. The UFO-nauts seized both men and glided back into the craft. Parker couldn't handle the eerie situation any longer and blacked out in a dead faint. The beings separated Hickson and Parker and began an examination of Hickson. He was suspended in mid-air as a big eye-shaped football-sized contraption snooped over his body. About twenty minutes later, the two abductees were deposited back on land and the UFO seemed to disappear instantaneously.

At first, Hickson and Parker didn't know what to do. Hickson was a little more composed than his young companion who was close to hysterics, although Hickson himself could remember little of the onboard adventure. Should they keep their experience a secret or report it? Finally, the anxiety, horror, and touch of excitement were too much for them and they reported their adventure to local officials.

Releasing the report was like opening floodgates. News reports jammed every media outlet from Maine to California. The press, TV talk shows, and documentary filmmakers all clamored for interviews with Hickson, whose domestic life became a greater ordeal than the UFO experience. Both Hickson and Parker were given polygraph (lie detector) examinations and came out clean as a whistle.

When I first read about the Pascagoula case, I wasn't impressed by it. As a psychic investigator by trade, I always look for telltale signs of a hoax whenever I read a new report. First I looked for outside witnesses to the Pascagoula case. Sure, I thought, there might have been outside witnesses to general UFO activity in the Pascagoula area, but did anyone actually see the object in the shipyard? No! The lack of an outside witness didn't bother me too much. Although witnesses are great for evidential purposes, lack of a corroborative witness to an event does not brand it a hoax. So, instead, I started to compare the abductees' stories, looking for loopholes or inconsistencies. It was then that I got turned off by the case. Parker's fainting spell looked awfully staged to me. If the two were pulling a hoax, they certainly would have studied up on the famous Betty and Barney Hill adventure to see what they would be in for. The most fascinating evidential aspect of the Hill case was the fact that the two victims reported consistent and identical stories when hypnotized and questioned independently. If Hickson and Parker were hoaxing either for publicity, money, or whatever, they had to be careful to keep their stories painstakingly consistent. This would be difficult, since they knew that they would be subjected to a grueling cross-examination at the hands of skeptics who would love to crack the story wide open. So what better way to get around the problem than by having Parker faint after the initial sighting, thus leaving Hickson as the sole witness? Using this ploy, Hickson had his independent witness, but not one who could foul things up later.

Well, that is how I analyzed the Pascagoula case in 1973. I didn't think any more about it until early 1975 when I received a call from Ralph Blum, author of a popular and best-selling UFO book *Beyond Earth: Man's Contact with UFOs*. I had seen the book on the stands and Blum himself on TV. I had been impressed by his knowledge and presence and was surprised to learn that he was working on a psychic book project. He had called to see if I could provide him with some information. Of course our conversation quickly turned to UFOs, and I expressed my misgivings about the Pascagoula testimony. I was in for a rude awakening. Blum had actually been in Pascagoula and was intimate with Hickson, Parker, and their families. Gradually, Blum gave me some information that was bound to put a new light on the case. He told me about the total disintegration of Hickson's private life, how Calvin Parker had been hospitalized after a complete nervous breakdown, how J. Allen Hynek had secretly seen Parker praying for guidance, and how a secret microphone caught private conversations between the two men. They were frightened, bewildered, and panicky conversations. Gradually my arm-chair criticisms of the Pascagoula case wilted. Blum kept hitting me with more and more inside information on the case—the other witnesses to the UFO activity that night, and Hickson's sincerity and lack of any sophisticated training, which he would have needed to pull off such a caper.

As Blum and I ended our telephone conversation, he said a few words which prompted me to reexamine the Pascagoula case in an attempt to find an explanation—Ufological or otherwise—for Hickson's and Parker's experience. After defending the two men, Blum said, "I don't know if their experience was a UFO one, telepathy, or what. I just know something happened."

The word "telepathy" hit me like a bullet. Why had Blum brought in a parapsychological concept? As I began reevaluating the case, I once again found evidence that a psychic mystery, as well as a Ufological one, had cast its shadow over Pascagoula that weird October day. Here is my new analysis.

The first mystery we have to contend with is one brought out by Blum himself in his book. As I mentioned in my description of the shipyard layout, a bridge bordered the pier on the left. According to Hickson's testimony, the UFO was huge and was within forty or so yards of them. This would have been in clear view from the bridge. Yet, as Blum writes:

> ... I have not been able to resolve ... the fact that the craft Charlie Hickson was "floated aboard" in Pascagoula was not reported by even one of the cars crossing the Highway 90 bridge, just a stone's throw from the old Shaupeter Shipyard. Nor was its arrival or departure recorded by the "zoomar security cameras" that Ingills Shipyard reportedly uses to scan the river at night. And yet according to Charlie Hickson he was aboard the craft some twenty to thirty minutes, and according to Dr. Hynek, Charlie's experience was "very real and frightening." But the truth is, we still don't know the exact nature of his experience.

Since the UFO encounter was late at night, drivers traversing the bridge might not have noted the UFO even though, according to Hickson, it emitted light.* But the failure of the security system to zero in on the object is a more bizarre feature. So we have to begin with the eye-opening premise that perhaps the UFO was not physically there at all. One solution to the Pascagoula mystery is given by Jerome Clark and Loren Coleman in their book *The Unidentified*. They suggest that Hickson and Parker had a "mutual nightmare" which was shared by telepathy. I can't support this explanation for several reasons. First, as I said in the last chapter, no evidence amassed in parapsychology has ever given credence to the theory that two people can share an exact telepathic rapport. Usually telepathic messages are distorted, fragmented, or symbolic. Now, there *is* a phenomenon called "mutual dreaming," in which two people do telepathically share dream content. But if you examine these cases of synchronous dreams, you will readily see that while dreams might share themes, symbols, or general content, they are not even close to being replicas. One sleeper might dream of catching a pi-

---

* Mr. Lucius Farish, the well-known American Ufologist, has recently communicated to me the fact that the shipyard cannot necessarily be seen from the bridge.

geon in a park, while the other might dream of catching fish, coming home and finding a pigeon flying in his house, etc. The dream *content* is there, but not a *replica* of the dream itself.

Another argument I have against the Clark-Coleman theory is based on the psychological reaction that the two men had to their experience. Nowhere in the literature of abnormal psychology, dream research, or clinical studies do I find even one case in which a dream led to such a deep-seated trauma or to an eventual breakdown of the sort Parker finally suffered. Dreams may reflect traumas or replay them, but they do not cause them. Also, one could ask Clark and Coleman: Why did Parker faint instead of sharing the rest of the "dream" with Hickson?

However, if Hickson were psychic, we have a plausible explanation for the events. Could he have built up a UFO fantasy that infected Parker? In other words, could the older man have somehow created an apparitional drama that objectified just enough to be experienced by Parker, yet not enough to be physically objective? The information parapsychology has amassed about apparitions does not rule out the possibility of just this sort of intricate drama. There are many cases on record in which several people have seen an apparition collectively, yet the phantom gave every indication of being nonobjective. For example, it merely faded away or walked through a wall, unlike a physical object. Somehow, in these cases, the psychic force that gave rise to the apparition was strong enough to infect everyone in the general area. So, I ask you, could the Hickson-Parker experience really be a giant psychic drama liberated by Hickson's psychic potential?

In order to support this theory, one would have to credit Hickson with amazing psychic abilities. Yet Hickson looks nothing like a great psychic. He is self-conscious, relatively uncultured, and claims to have little psychic background. But while talking to Ralph Blum, Hickson unknowingly dropped the key—a key with which we can unlock the Pascagoula case. During an interview, Blum had asked Hickson why he didn't wear a wristwatch. Hickson dropped the bomb when he answered:

> "Never could. People said I had electricity. To give you an example, before I went into the service, I tried two or three wristwatches. But they wouldn't keep time on me. They'd either lose time, or gain time. Or they'd just stop. Then, after I went to Asia, we captured North Korean and Chinese, and

they'd have pockets full of watches they'd taken off of the G.I.s they'd probably killed. Well, I said to myself, I'm just gonna see now, and I tried every make and brand that I could find, but I never did find one that would keep correct time. I even tried these Elgins, these railroad pocket watches. And they won't keep correct time. So I don't tote a watch."

Blum overlooked these remarks completely in his book. He doesn't give them a second thought. Yet they are probably the most significant remarks Hickson made in any of his interviews. The failure of his watch to function indicates psychokinesis. Some psychics, such as Uri Geller and another psychic with whom I have worked, claim that watches refuse to work when kept in too close contact with them. Hickson's claim is more than a story. It is clear that he tested all sorts of watches to find one that would keep time. None did. It is hard to come up with a normal explanation for this timepiece highjinx. Psychokinesis is left as the most plausible explanation. So, as we read Hickson's words, another disturbing thought comes to mind—that beneath his hesitant and frightened facade, Charlie Hickson might be harboring a storehouse of psychic energy just waiting to be released.

The likelihood that Hickson has psychokinetic abilities makes the Pascagoula case a whole new ball game. Instead of being victimized by an interstellar UFO, he could have projected a psychic "sphere of influence" over the shipyard which was partly physical and party subjective, and in which Parker found himself captive. Parker's faint may have been more than the result of fright. In the case of Dr. X., it looked as if the doctor used his PK ability to withdraw energy not only from himself but from his young child. Could Hickson have withdrawn psychic energy from young Parker to help create the drama? The great physical mediums of the nineteenth and twentieth centuries, who could levitate tables and create phantom presences, all entered a trance before the phenomena manifested or after the initial psychokinetic displays broke out. For some reason, only when immobilized by trance could they eject their psychic powers. Parker's fainting spell as the drama reached its climax and denouement may actually have been an enforced trance as power was withdrawn from him to "fuel the fire," so to speak. And what of the spacecraft itself? Remember, Hickson said it seemed to disappear almost the moment that he came around from the ordeal. The UFO activity which was prevalent that night could have served as the prototype suggestion from which Hickson molded the terrifying drama.

As the days went by, Hickson's mind seemed to be drawn closer and closer to the October 11th encounter. He told Blum that after the experience was over, it wasn't as if his previously paralyzed body was re-animating. It was more as though his *mind* was returning to normal. This, in itself, is a provocative and suggestive statement. But then he continued, "... You know at night I lie in bed and I think about them. ... If I can, I think I'd *like* to get in touch with them. I mean it. Every night when I'm in bed, it's almost a picture comes into my mind. Just the same way every time ... I'm not in the picture. Just them. They're not doing anything. They're not inside the ship, they're just *there*. All I have to do is close my eyes.

Again these are exceptionally revealing words, for Hickson is vaguely telling us the real story behind Pascagoula. The spacecraft and the UFO-nauts are not flying the heavens or exploring the seas. The UFO and its occupants have gone right into Hickson's mind—right back into the recesses that gave them birth.

Very few people have followed up the subsequent career of Charlie Hickson. The Pascagoula case is now a classic, and Hickson and Parker are just two more names in the annals of UFO reports. The public and the press have very short memories. However, in trying to trace Hickson's subsequent career and experiences, we find even more evidence for my psychic theory about the Pascagoula mystery.

On October 11, 1974, which was the first anniversary of the Pascagoula sighting, Hickson, accompanied by a friend, returned to the pier, "... kinda hopin' you know, that they would come back . . ." Nothing happened. The next day Hickson and his friend, Professor William Mendez, flew to Austin, Texas, to be the guests of Project Starlight International, a UFO-investigating organization which is under the direction of Ray Stanford, who is himself a psychic and a UFO witness. P.S.I. has a special UFO tracking rig set up in the Texas countryside which includes photographic equipment and a huge circular formation of lights that can signal overhead vehicles.

At 8:59 P.M., as Stanford, Hickson, and several others were at the site, a brilliant disc-like object flew overhead. It was orangish green with a beam of light projecting downward from its underside. As Stanford reported, "Hickson's reaction left some of those present with the subjective feeling that he was pleased to be seeing something strange, but was not nearly as startled as the others present—as if he had already seen or experienced something much more startling at an earlier time."

Hickson's P.S.I. sighting is even more coincidental than the Sanderson–Keel encounter described in the last chapter. Coincidence is hard put to explain the fact that Hickson, Stanford, and several others should all see a UFO (1) just as they were showing Hickson their tracking devices, and (2) within twenty-four hours of the first anniversary of the Pascagoula case. Once again, I believe Hickson was actually creating the objects they all saw.

The last word on UFO abductions has not yet been said, however. Even today, as we are just beginning to get to the core of the Charlie Hickson experience, another case has cropped up which is even more bizarre and disturbing.

Twenty-two-year-old Travis Walton was abducted by a UFO near Heber, Arizona, on November 5, 1976. Unlike the Hickson case, though, when Travis disappeared there were five witnesses! Walton was one of a group of tree-trimmers that included Swayne Smith, Kenneth Peterson, Alan Dalis, Mike Rogers, and John Goulette. All of them were under thirty years of age. It was dusk and the boys were driving on a deserted mountain byway when the crew spotted a UFO hovering over a clearing beside the road.

"I was numb with disbelief—and terrifed," Smith told reporters. "The UFO was giving off a yellowish orange light."

Travis jumped out of the truck to take a closer look at the vehicle and walked right underneath it. "He walked beneath the saucer," Smith continued, "then a blue ray shot down from the saucer and he just vanished!"

The next several moments were sheer pandemonium. Mike Rogers, the driver, gunned the truck past the saucer. A safe distance away, he stopped and everyone jumped out, shouting at one another in terror. A flash among the trees silenced them for the moment—the saucer had blasted off. Subsequently all the crew took lie-detector tests and passed with flying colors. Navajo County Sheriff Marlin Gillespie, who interviewed the boys, could only mumble, "I've been in law enforcement for eighteen sears and I've never known anything like it."

Walton showed up five days later. He was dehydrated,

dumbfounded, and had an odd puncture wound on his right arm. Beyond a dim recollection of the UFO encounter, he couldn't recall most of what had happened. He suddenly found himself about eight miles away from where he had been abducted; he ran to town and called his relatives.

As is typical of abduction cases, hypnosis was used to help unclog the victim's memory. The hypnotist was Dr. James Harder, whose work was supervised by three physicians and a psychiatrist. Under hypnosis, Walton told his interviewers that after blacking out he awoke blurry-eyed and aching from head to chest. At first he thought he was in a hospital, but gradually he became aware of humanoid figures bending over him. Walton could only describe them as looking like "well-developed fetuses" wrapped in robes. Walton jumped up instinctively, but before he could attack the abductors, he blacked out again.

Of course, this whole story could be a hypnotic fantasy, as Patrolman Schirmer's story appears to be. Dr. Jean Rosenbaum, chairman of the Southwest Psychoanalytic Association, who witnessed the hypnotic session, preferred to think that ". . . he suffered from a combination of imagination and amnesia—that he did not go up on a UFO but simply was wandering around during his disappearance."

One wonders, though, how convinced Rosenbaum is, for he added, "But I'm unable to account for five witnesses having the same story and passing the lie-detector tests."

And neither can I. As I said earlier, the last word has not yet been spoken about UFO abduction cases, even taking psychic phenomena into account. What happened on November 5, 1975, in Arizona? Did Walton and his friends participate in a group apparitional drama? Or did Walton step into a very real flying saucer? There is no doubt in my mind that some UFOs are psychic projections. But I also said that no theory is 100 percent correct. The Walton case is one of those damned exceptions to the rule that keeps everybody wondering—and we will be wondering for years to come.

CHAPTER 6
The Cosmic Invaders

I do not know exactly my age when I had my first Satanic experience. As near as I can say I was six or seven. I was lying in bed when I felt drawn and horrified by a presence outside my bedroom. I rose from my bed, magnetised by the unseen horror, and opened the door of my room. What I saw was unforgettable. I first noticed his face. It was smaller than a human's but it's proportions were the same. It was covered with a close-woven blue-grey pelt. A blue light issued from it. The colour, the aura, the clinging fur were nothing compared to the evil of his smile. His smile was not only diabolic but welcoming. His body was like a man's but more slenderly made and his height was less.

His body was bent forward in an ingratiating posture. From head to foot he was covered with the same blue-grey pelt and everywhere a bluish aura emanated from him. His legs were different. He did not have human feet. His legs tapered down to what appeared to be slender stumps, but I was so hypotized by his face and his evil smile that I did not look closely at his feet. I know now that he had hooves.

I do not know how I got back to my bed. I am not sure if it was the same night that my obsession began, but certainly it was very soon after. I knelt to say my prayers. Then, after I had got to bed, I got out again immediately. I knelt and prayed and returned to bed. I did this innumerable times. I went on until I stayed in bed from sheer exhaustion and could no longer make the effort to rise from it.

This is a perfect obsessional ritual and there is nothing startling about its nature and intent. What is important is that it supervened so soon after the experience which precipitated it. I felt myself in the presence of great evil. I went towards it, felt it, and it made an indelible impression on me. I responded to evil not by guilt but by sheer, naked panic . . .

Although this narrative reads like something out of a fifteenth-century witchcraft trial, it was actually written in 1972 by Dr. Arthur Guirdham, one of England's leading psychiatrists.

Dr. Guirdham is certainly unique among physicians. He is not only a psychiatrist but a natural mystic as well. Born in 1905, he first studied medicine at Oxford University, which he left after completing his studies in 1927 to take up clinical studies at Charing Cross Hospital in London. Guirdham was medical superintendent of Bailbrook House, Bath, from 1935–68, and since retiring has served on a National Health Service committee whose function it is to nominate psychiatric candidates to its ranks.

Dr. Guirdham is no slouch. He is a highly regarded and trained mental health specialist who was a practicing clinician for some forty years. However, there is one element of his approach to psychiatry that makes him unique among behavorial scientists. He believes that the world is haunted by evil forces and that these forces can exert a wicked pressure on unsuspecting man. And in 1972 he wrote a book, *Obsession*, in which he assembled all his evidence.

In the previous chapter, I pointed out that our psyches are capable of creating all sorts of apparitional dramas. UFOs are certainly not the only phantoms that invade our universe. Now, there is nothing inherently evil about UFOs. Even abductees rarely come to the conclusion that their hosts were malicious or wicked. But poltergeist cases, on the other hand, would seem to indicate that man can unleash a vindictive energy molded by the will. Are there other types of even more wicked forces in the universe? Can evil become a physical or psychic energy, and are we releasing such a nefarious power into the world around us?

Dr. Guirdham is one of the few modern thinkers who has studied these possibilities in depth. During his years as a clinician, he gradually began realizing that many of the night terrors his adolescent patients reported were not psychological afflictions but were instead reactions to evil forces which they had sensed around them. As the psychiatrist wryly commented in his book, "... at the Child Guidance Clinic I found to what degree other children had night terrors. It took me fifty years to discover what they meant."

Guirdham's theory about the ontogenesis of night terrors is bold, and I doubt if very many other mental health workers would share his views:

These night terrors are among the child's first contact with evil on the psychic plane; certainly they are psychic as well as psychological phenomena. The child sees them because, generally speaking, he is more receptive than the adult to psychic experience. This is because in his earlier years the psyche and the personality are more loosely attached to each other than in later life. The former is freer to operate because it is not yet rendered insensitive by the rigid development of the carapace of personality. These hallucinations occur at night because, on going to sleep, the contact between psyche and personality is loosened still further.

This is certainly a provocative theory, but Guirdham goes even further with it:

It is only natural that the principalities and powers of darkness should assemble round the bed of a child at night. It is only at an early age that the majority can receive the imprint of evil from night terrors. As we grow and are educated, our capacity for idea formation is developed at the expense of perception. It is only natural that the energy of evil should attack us at the age of innocence.

One such victim who came to Guirdham's attention was a little nine-year-old girl. The child was living a nightmare. Her body twitched convulsively, and she kept crying out "No!" to any question Guirdham addressed to her. Eventually the "no's" were addressed to an invisible presence and turned into obscene exclamations. By delving into her clinical history, the psychiatrist discovered that this obsessive response had begun long before, after a particularly disturbing nightmare. Guirdham could uncover no psychiatric reason for her affliction and came to the conclusion that the nightmare represented a very real psychic attack. Her puzzling speech, he concluded, was the girl's feeble attempt to ward off the evil.

Dr. Guirdham came across an even more provocative case when he started treating a hyperkinetic four-year-old boy. The child had been hyperactive since birth. Yet, while psychologically disturbed, the lad had a remarkably developed intellectual prowess. His vocabulary and means of expression, for example, astounded Guirdham. The hyperkinesis eventually led the boy to form an obsessive compulsive ritual. Every night he would spend time ritualistically walking about the house. It took Guirdham three years to discover the cause.

By working with his young patient for session after session,

Guirdham finally uncovered the fact that the boy's earliest childhood memory was of an apparitional visitor. All through his young life he had been visited by similar threatening phantoms. His nightly wanderings, Guirdham came to believe, had no psychiatric basis but were attempts to escape the evil brought by the entities.

As I hinted previously, not all psychiatrists are going to look favorably upon Dr. Guirdham's rather unconventional views about the nature of night terrors. They certainly contradict many conventional ideas about the genesis of childhood obsession-compulsions. (The most widely accepted theory about these rituals is that they represent the child's attempts to cope with guilt.) How good an argument for the existence of evil do Guirdham's cases present? One answer has been given by Dr. Ian Stevenson, a psychiatrist and parapsychologist at the University of Virginia, who stated in a review of Guirdham's *Obsession* which appeared in the July, 1974, issue of the *Journal of the American Society for Psychical Research*:

> But where is the evidence to support Dr. Guirdham's more sweeping generalization which would account for a large block of psychiatric patients on the basis of a special vulnerability to psychical communication? It is certainly not in this book. The author gives fewer than a dozen case histories in any detail and he summarizes even these in a way which makes it difficult for the reader to form independent judgments about the patients, their symptoms, and Dr. Guirdham's interpretations.

So, it seems that even seasoned psychiatrists will often be at loggerheads when they confront the issue of evil and how it affects man in his daily life. Who is right, Dr. Guirdham, who sees evil as a force striving for expression through human victims, or Dr. Stevenson, who sees this view as a fantasy in itself?

I first became fascinated with the possibility that evil is a genuine psychic force several years ago when my colleague Raymond Bayless told me about a strange encounter he had shared with his brother. When they were teen-agers they had once found themselves face to face with an invisible evil presence right in their own home! Both felt it and both reacted with sheer panic. Bayless, like Guirdham, now believes, on the basis of his experience, that evil is not a moral issue but a physical reality. Here is Bayless's story as he recounted it to me:

The Cosmic Invaders

In 1938 I experienced an unusual and frightening adventure along with my brother. Our family was living in Denver. We had arrived home one evening only to find no one there. I remained dowstairs after entering the house, while my brother went upstairs. At this time I suddenly realized that something hideous and evil was in the house. There was no logical reason for my receiving this impression, it was a totally spontaneous impression. This impression was so forceful and disturbing that I could not help but run out the back door to escape outside. As I ran, I almost collided into my brother. He was bolting downstairs and was also heading for the door! Outside at last, we compared notes. To my surprise, my brother told me that while upstairs he had been overpowered by the horrible feeling that there was something evil in the house. He, too, had had the urge to run from the house in order to escape from it. Even to this day, I have no explanation to account for this strange experience. Suffice it to say that no normal explanation can account for the fact that both my brother and myself had identical impressions while in different parts of the house.

This is certainly a curious experience. While I have, of course, heard of people with "free-floating anxiety," I've never heard of a case where two people shared the attack. I can only think of two possible explanations for the experience. The first is, simply, that one of the Baylesses had a momentary delusion which was instantly transferred to the other telepathically. The second explanation is that there really was something intangible but dreadful in the house.

Now, we have to ask ourselves which of these explanations fits the facts better. And of course we also have to ask if this case can be explained psychologically at all.

The only phenomenon known to clinical psychology which in any way resembles Bayless' experiences is an anxiety attack. Douglas De Nike and Norman Tiber, in their chapter on neurotic behavior in Perry London's and Davis Rosenham's textbook, *Foundations of Abnormal Psychology*, have this to say about anxiety attacks:

> Anxiety attacks are characterized by chronic, infocused, or "free-floating" fear, which varies in its intensity. This victim appears tense in both posture and facial expression and may report physical discomfort. He seems "jumpy," with hair-trigger reflexes, as if ready to react to some unknown danger. He is afraid of everything and nothing all at once. For some

people in anxiety states, this background of chronic distress is periodically punctuated by attacks of stark terror...

This description doesn't fit Bayless too well. First, he reports no history of anxiety. When he had walked into the house that fateful evening he was as carefree as possible. Now anxiety attacks which lead to panic reactions are suffered by people who have long histories of neurotic anxiety. This, in fact, serves as the background for their attacks. Secondly, and this is an important point, Bayless' fears focused on something present in the house although he could see nothing. Anxiety panic is *not* focused; the victim has literally no idea why he has been suddenly struck by fear. So the anxiety-attack theory just can't apply to this case. Moreover, how could Bayless' alleged anxiety have tranferred itself to his brother upstairs? Telepathy is an unlikely explanation. Both simultaneously developed the exact feelings of fear and panic and both felt that something in the house was responsible, causing them to react in the very same way. And even if the incident was mediated by telepathy, what served to ignite the original fear?

I think we have to conclude that Raymond Bayless actually did confront something evil, something from which he knew he must escape. This loathsome thing was only ephemeral, however. When the Bayless brothers ventured to reenter the house later that evening, its atmosphere was perfectly normal.

I can personally attest to the fact that these feelings of panic can be very real. I had a similar encounter myself in 1973 under rather peculiar circumstances, to say the least!

I was residing in a haunted house at the time. I had previously lived through two separate outbreaks there, so I wasn't at all nervous about spending another night in the house. In fact, I had spent over 750 perfectly peaceful nights there. But that one night in 1973 was to be different from any other I have ever experienced. Usually the haunting would act up every few months or so in the evenings or at night. However, at the time of this rather curious incident, the house was going through one of its dry spells.

I had gone to bed about 1:00 in the morning. I'm not a very sound sleeper and wake up often in the course of a night. That particular night I awoke suddenly with the feeling that "something" was watching me from the wall against which I had shoved my bed. I don't know what this "something" was, all I know is that I had a horrible obsession that *I must escape from the room.* By the time I finally realized what was happening, I had already jumped from the bed and run through the door and was standing in the middle of the den. All of these reactions took place in the twinkling of an eye. I reentered the room wondering what could have caused me to literally panic upon wakening from sleep. Whatever "it" was, it had gone and I went sleepily but nervously back to bed.

Never in my life have I ever had a similar experience. Nor can it be argued that I merely "suggested" the reaction because I knew the house was haunted. That explanation is sheer nonsense since I had lived in the house for two years without ever experiencing anything like that before. It was just as though someone had yelled, "Escape!"

Sometimes this type of evil does not invade or seek to possess some weak mortal, but instead permeates an entire area. The evil becomes affixed to a certain location in space, just as a haunting does. One of these zones of evil cropped up in the Ohio Valley during a 1967 UFO-monster flap. John Keel, the veteran Ufologist, was on the scene investigating the reports when he stumbled across the zone:

> It was well past midnight as I drove aimlessly up and down the dirt roads among the igloos ... as I passed a certain point on one of the isolated roads I was suddenly engulfed in fear. I stepped on the gas and after I went a few yards my fear vanished as quickly as it came. I continued to drive, eventually returning again to the same spot. And again a wave of unspeakable fear swept over me. I drove quickly away from the place and then stopped puzzled. Why would this one stretch of road produce this hair-raising effect?

Keel drove back to the spot and, sure enough, he was once again overcome by panic as he drove through it. His curiosity piqued by his little discovery, the investigator got out of his car and proceeded to explore the region on foot. He walked slowly toward the zone, and then—as soon as he stepped into it—his panic and fear suddenly returned. The next day the zone was gone.

Keel tried to explain away the zone, rationalizing that ultrasonic waves were probably saturating the accursed area and causing his peculiar reaction. But where did the waves come from? "I searched for power transmission lines, telephone microwave towers, and anything that might have radiated energy through the area. There was nothing," Keel admitted.

Keel is not the only adventurer who has stumbled across these hotbeds of evil. An almost identical zone was discovered halfway around the world by the English writer, Tom Lethbridge, in 1962.

As Lethbridge explains in his book, *Ghost and Divining Rod*, he and his wife were collecting seaweed at Lodram Bay to use as compost. While on their little expedition, they discovered a specific area on the beach which caused them to lapse into a deep depression and fear.

"I can't stand this place any longer," exclaimed his wife. "I think there's something frightful here."

Each of the two beachcombers had independently had the same oppressive feeling in the area, and they hurriedly fled from the scene.

The next week, the Lethbridges returned to the beach in order to further explore the eerie zone. They found it with little difficulty and discovered that the intense feelings they experienced there seemed to focus around a small stream that ran onto the beach. Lethbridge's wife couldn't stand the feeling the area generated, so she wandered off and hiked up a hill. But the evil even followed her there. As she mounted a cliff to look over the terrain below, something invisible but intensely powerful tried to force her to jump off.

There are striking coincidences between Keel's and the Lethbridge's experiences. All three felt the evil localized in space; they all discovered that they could step in and out of the zone; and they all found it nearly impossible to expose themselves to the area's influence for a long period of time.

Very similar infestations have been known to focus on a house. Far from traditional hauntings, which are placid and ephemeral, these cases are vicious and malevolent. They are not typical hauntings. They represent a virtual invasion of a house by an evil force.

Two people who were unfortunate enough to find themselves trapped in one of these nests of evil were Esther Le Leau and her husband, who wrote up their account for the *Journal of the American Society for Psychical Research* in 1951. It is one of the most disturbing and detailed accounts on the power of evil ever written.

The nightmare started for the Le Leaus, a young married couple with two children and a baby on the way, in 1930. The Reverend Le Leau and his wife, Esther, were looking

The Cosmic Invaders 143

forward to finding a home to move into at the time. Finally they found just what they were looking for in a nice Oklahoma town—a big, two-story house, shaded by trees, and sporting a large southern-style back porch.

The very day they moved in, the couple had their first ominous warning that something was wrong in the house. Their son Ernie had been romping around the house when he admitted to his mother in a puzzled voice: "I don't *like* that room," He pointed to an upstairs bedroom. "There's a goat in that closet."

"Don't be silly," reponded Mrs. Le Leau, fully aware that the five-year-old boy was trying to say "ghost."

However, Mrs. Le Leau had the same uneasy feelings that her son had voiced. She too could feel a disturbing influence which emanated from the stairwell. This influence began to prey on her nerves. It grew and grew, and finally the young housewife found herself ritually praying over the beds of her children to protect them from it. As she explained:

> In a number of weeks, I became so afraid that evenings I would move the baby's little crib into the study, which was upstairs at the end of the hall and was seemingly *protected* from the "menace," and take Dorey and Ernie in there to play until they became sleepy. Then when I heard my husband's car drive up, to scramble madly to pop them into their Bible-protected beds in their own room and greet him with a face—a face which he in time noticed was getting thinner and more hollow-eyed.

Mrs. Le Leau eventually became so afflicted by the house that she had to undergo medical treatments. Nothing helped though; the young wife could feel the "menace," as she called it, growing and growing in intensity:

> As the evening hours progressed, it grew stronger, until finally, I could time its actual arrive—10 P.M., exactly, it would be in the house waiting. And as the intensity grew and its animosity grew, the more clearly I could "see" it without seeing it—a tall, dark faceless shrouded presence, utterly evil, utterly vile. Just waiting and waiting and hating, there in the hall. And I would either sit in the study, or lie wide-awake in bed also waiting and waiting and *willing* that *I'd not give way to fear*, for I knew if ever I did, all was lost.

It was at this time that Mrs. Le Leau found out that her minister husband also felt the presence in the house. Until that time, she had kept her horror to herself, not wishing to alarm him. But suddenly it became clear to her—her husband had independently felt the presence at night himself.

The evil would even follow a predictable pattern. It seemed to emanate from a cistern under the house; it would rise up over the porch roof and enter the upstairs hallway either through their bedroom window or the bathroom window. But it had an aversion to light. According to Mrs. Le Leau:

> You could feel it creeping. Later I could "see" it standing in the hall. Vile. Evil. With a horrible repulsiveness that made your mind crawl. Sometimes, I thought that there was a terrible stench. My husband agrees to this, too. But as long as there was a light, and I did not yield to *fear*, it was helpless. But promptly, and my husband verifies to this too, at 2 A.M., with the suddenness of the click of a light switch, it was gone and we could go to sleep. The danger was over until the next night.

As the evil progressed, Mrs. Le Leau found herself caught up in a obsessive-compulsive ritual. She would ritualistically place Bibles all through the house. She was like a madwoman, caught up in the frenzy of her own delusions. But this oppressing fear was no delusion. The fact that her husband experienced it as well more than indicated that some psychic entity was stalking the couple.

Actually, Mrs. Le Leau's frantic obsession about placing the Bibles throughout the house is exactly in line with some of Dr. Guirdham's views. As I mentioned at the onset of this chapter, Guirdham believes that night terrors and obsessive compulsive acts are not necessarily the result of psychological problems but can be intuitive reactions to psychic attack and evil. Although a conventional psychiatrist would probably have diagnosed Mrs. Le Leau as an obsessive-compulsive neurotic with paranoid delusions, we can see that her experiences go much deeper than any psychiatric labeling. Mrs. Le Leau was fighting evil the only way she knew how.

Predictably, the Le Leaus finally resolved to move from the dreadful place only three months after they had moved in. Mrs. Le Leau had wasted to a mere skeleton of her former self, her husband couldn't sleep without being tormented by nightmares, and the two could no longer sleep upstairs without being overcome by the intruder. The presence knew that its victims wanted to escape, and it decided to pay them a final, mocking farewell. As Mrs. Le Leau explained:

We found a house in a matter of a few days, and were all packed, ready to move the next day except for my husband's books in the study. He was packing them the last night. I had grown so afraid in the house, I was even afraid for him to be up there alone doing that, and kept an ever apprehensive ear open for his cheery whistling. It grew later and later, and my apprehensions grew. His whistling had ceased, but I could hear him moving about. But the silence settled down and the whole house seemed to wait, and horror and terror and danger swept through the house all at once like a tide. There was a crashing rush of feet on the stairs, the door was literally hurled open, and my husband, white and panting, flung into the room. "My God," he gasped, "That damned thing came into the study just now."

The Le Leaus moved the same day.

Mrs. Le Leau waited some twenty years before writing about her experiences. Yet, through those years she lived under the constant shadow of the evil which had tormented her for a bare three months. Her report ends on a note of utter despair:

> Four months later we moved out of the state. Ten years later we moved to another state. And then years later to another. But no matter where we have lived, we have always burned a night light because of the horror and the terror we experienced at L——— Street.

A very similar type of haunting was recorded by Jan Bryant Bartell in her recent book, *Spindrift*. Mrs. Bartell wasn't much of a believer in the supernatural until she moved into a big brownstone townhouse on 10th Street in New York City's colorful Greenwich Village. At first, nothing unusual happened in the house, but gradually Mrs. Bartell became aware of a alien presence there. Ghostly shadows flitted across the room, animals acted oddly in the house, weird noises invaded her privacy, and finally Mrs. Bartell found herself engulfed by a vile force. Parapsychologists could not explain it, and mediums didn't seem able to exorcise it.

Eventually Mrs. Bartell moved next door . . . but the evil pervaded the neighboring building as well. Ultimately people who lived near the accursed apartment began to die. There was nothing unusual about the deaths—cancer, accidents, and so forth—but they struck down, one after another, the people who lived near or often visited the 10th Street townhouse. Mrs. Bartell finally realized that a psychic curse afflicted the building and she fled from Greenwich Village, hoping to rid herself of the haunting and every foul thing associated with it. But she, too, died just after finishing her book. Was she the house's final victim? Did the evil that infested the house cling to her even after she fled? Mrs. Bartell's book, *Spindrift*, was her own obituary.

What was the force that attacked the Le Leaus and Mrs. Bartell, which confronted the Bayless brothers, and over whose depraved domain Keel and the Lethbridges trespassed? There is no doubt in my mind that these cases all but prove that evil can become a concrete psychic force in the world. In fact, I believe that there might actually be two kinds of evil forces that can haunt us. First, some totally independent evil force may exist in the world ... a primordial evil that compulsively seeks to destroy. There might also be an evil force lurking within our own minds. Many intuitive writers and philosophers have toyed with this idea, and I believe that the fruit of their wisdom is not just idle speculation. Robert Louis Stevenson, for example, wrote his famous story, *Dr. Jekyll and Mr. Hyde*, to illustrate that evil can lurk even within the most noble and compassionate person. What is even more unsettling, Stevenson suggests that this evil is constantly striving for expression. The horror behind the Nazi movement, the crimes against humanity we read about in the papers daily, the horrors that lead to war, even the religious slaughters of post-Reformation Europe—these are all manifestations of the evil that hides behind man's noble facade.

Now, I am tempted to ask, what if this evil leaves the mind and body and becomes an independent entity with its own intelligence and volition, just as the poltergeist seems to develop? The poltergeist represents a distructive force within man's mind. But it takes a poor second place to the horror of projected psychic evil. One can only wonder what would have happened if the Le Leaus had not fled.

Miracles prove that our planet is haunted by powers of good. UFOs demonstrate that our world plays host to a force that seeks to mystify us. But let us not be lulled into a false security. There are many evil things invading this tiny planet of ours, and this evil is a physical reality. And sometimes, I'm afraid to admit, it focuses right on us.

CHAPTER 7
A Psychic Look at Forteana

My purpose in this book has been to show that many mysteries of nature and the universe are actually psychic phenomena. But there are mysteries that go beyond the paranormal, mysteries we can only explain or try to explain by the wildest speculation.

These are the very mysteries that Charles Fort began to collect at the close of the nineteenth century. By carefully hoarding news releases, investigating back issues of papers, and perusing scientific publications, Fort eventually amassed hundreds of "impossible" events: reports of unknown objects in the sky and in the sea; rains of rocks and rains of blood; teleported people and apporting poltergeists; flaming people and watery monsters; unknown things that fell from the sky and bizarre objects fround buried beneath the ground. Fort called these events "the damned" since they were condemned as being impossible by science—condemned because science had no explanation for them. Today we call these phenomena "Forteana" in honor of the man who first brought them to our attention.

Why are these phenomena damned even today, when science itself is liberalizing its views about the world, the universe, and man's potential? Perhaps it is because of the very nature of mystery. We love mystery, but only if a clue is left behind to help us solve it, as in an Agatha Christie novel. Forteana leave no clues. They are totally mysterious and singular events. They crop up now and then, and disappear just as mysteriously. It is as if nature had carried out the perfect crime. Science cannot even begin to examine Fortean phenomena analytically. All it can do is mimic what Aristotle did years ago—collect, collect, and collect specimens and hope that eventually some sense can be made out of the whole.

Psychic studies offer the only possible clue to understanding any Fortean phenomenon. As I said above, some Fortean events are definitely aberrant manifestations of psychic forces. How well does this explain all Fortean events? The following is a taxonomy of the main types of Fortean phenomena, or at least the manifestations collected and analyzed by Fortean experts: (1) strange things seen in the sky (UFOs, lights, strange planets); (2) things that fall from the sky (rains of odd objects, metal or slime seem to fall out of the heavens); (3) new animal forms (abominable snowmen, sea serpents, the Loch Ness monster); (4) remnants of unknown civilizations (ancient astronauts, Atlantis, misplaced objects such as the many ancient Chinese seals that were once found in England); (5) "wild talents" (including poltergeist, teleportations, spontaneous combustion, people who vanish forever); and (6) bizarre forces of nature (the Bermuda Triangle, animal anomalies, "extinct" animals surviving today).

Quite an assortment! One could easily spend a lifetime studying any one of these categories. Yet most of these mysteries can easily be explained as paranormal manifestations. We have already shown how UFOs and lights in the sky appear to be psychic projections of the mind. Rainfalls of objects are too similar to the type of falls recorded during poltergeist cases to be dismissed. Poltergeists often hurl rocks and assorted objects at the houses they persecute; so rains of fish, frogs or lizards may be just an odd form of poltergeist plague. Materialization and dematerialization could account for vanishing people; objects that fall from the sky and objects inexplicably found buried in the earth may have a common source. All these assorted anomalies may be the products of the psychic capabilities of the human mind. The mind that releases the poltergeist is also the mind that causes rocks to fall from the sky, people to vanish, and UFOs to appear.

Even "monsters" may manifest a psychic component, and this is what I would like to focus on now.

Down through man's history all sorts of aberrant life-forms have been recorded. A partial list of the reports alone would include giant men and animals; midgets and giants who appear by or out of UFOs; modern reports of dinosaurs (!); abominable snowmen and the American Bigfoot; men-in-black who mysteriously persecute UFO witnesses and show

A Psychic Look at Forteana

paranormal knowledge of their experiences and activities; winged manlike monsters; sea serpents, etc.

Obviously, some of these sightings are of mysterious but biologically normal animals. The Sasquach and Bigfoot are possible examples. Yet, other creatures are more mysterious. They appear and vanish out of and into nowhere, sometimes right before the eyes of astonished witnesses, and never leave any traces behind. They even show evidence of having psychic aptitudes. So when confronting the legend and lore of monsters, we may be dealing with two categories of events: physical creatures and apparitional or psychic beings.

It was only after I had come to this conclusion on my own that I discovered that veteran monster-hunter John Keel was of the same opinion. In his excellent compendium on monsters, *Strange Creatures from Time and Space*, he even classified them into two categories:

> The Group 1 type is, as we said, an animal—or even several different kinds of animals—still unknown to science. It is hostile only when threatened or attacked. It seems to be intelligent, perhaps it even has a high order of intelligence— as high, say, as that of the dolphin. This intelligence has made it almost as elusive and cunning as man himself. The footprints and other physical evidence accumulated over the years lend further credence to the eyewitness testimony. This creature exists. But he does not want anything to do with man. And who can blame him?
>
> Group 2 comprise the real mystery. They appear and disappear suddenly, as if they never existed at all. They rarely leave footsteps or other physical evidence behind. They seem to be more in the nature of paranormal or paraphysical apparitions. They attack people and automobiles, causing scratches, bruises, and black eyes. They chase cars and carry off cattle. They scream like banshees (maybe they are the original banshees of folklore), and despite their great height, weight, and girth, they melt into nothingness when the posses turn out. Since our data is admittedly only a fragment of all the sightings, we cannot guess at how long this has been going on, or what the real scope of the phenomenon is.

Like Keel, our attention also will be focused on Group 2 sightings. If Group 1 creatures are physically real, then they contribute little to our understanding of Forteana and psychic events. However, Group 2 monsters could be a breakthrough in our understanding of the forces of nature.

As far as I can see, there are three psychic explanations for these bizarre animals. The first would be that they are psychic projections just as are UFOs, miracles, and poltergeists. Something from us "projects out," takes on a physical form and a vestige of intelligence, and then disappears as the force which gave it birth dissipates. A second explanation is offered by John Keel, who suggests that these beings are intelligences in their own right and that "they" cause "us" to see them in a variety of forms. Or, Keel also suggests, they are free-floating, mindless masses of energy which take on a more finite shape when a human mind views them. A third theory would postulate that they might actually be ultra-dimensional entities which every so often get trapped in our world or travel via some interface between this world and another. Each of these theories does have some supporting evidence.

When I first theorized that monsters might be psychic projections similar in nature to UFOs and poltergeists, I also predicted to myself that monster appearances would be accompanied by odd electrical anomalies. As I showed earlier, poltergeists and UFOs have an absolute penchant for disrupting everything electrical, from cars to TV sets. A search through the literature on creature sightings did turn up two cases. One of then is a rather striking confirmation of my prediction; the other is weak and can easily be explained normally.

W. C. Priestly was driving home through Monongahela National Forest in October, 1960. His car was running fine but suddenly began to sputter and stall. As he told reporters of the Charleston, West Virginia, *Daily Mail,* "To my left side beside the road stood this monster with long hair pointing straight up toward the sky." Priestly was following a bus loaded with friends at the time. The eerie encounter came to a close when the bus turned around to ascertain why Priestly was no longer directly to the rear.

"It seemed this monster was very much afraid of the bus, dropped his hair (which was standing on end) and to my surprise as soon as he did this, my car started to run again," Priestly added.

No doubt shaken by the incident, Priestly began to follow the bus again, but sparks started flying out from under the hood of his car, as though the engine was shorting out. He peeked about the road nervously, and, as he half-expected, the creature was standing by the road once more. Later he discovered that the points of his car had been completely ruined by the encounter.

A Psychic Look at Forteana 151

One cannot dismiss the similarity between this report and the many electrical anomalies recorded during UFO sightings. There are many UFO reports which tell how the flying discs caused cars to stall or sputter during the duration of the sighting, but which ran again smoothly once the UFO had vanished. If Priestly's inquisitive friend was a physical object, such as a rather motley bear, there is no reason for its synergistic effect on the automobile. However, if, as I feel, the monster was a psychic projection akin to many UFOs, Priestly or the force behind the creature may have drawn energy from the car's ignition system to create it.

A second case is much less evidential. It occurred in Yakima, Washington, on September 19, 1966. Ken Pettijohn was just driving around a bend in the road when he saw a huge manlike creature covered by silvery hair standing in the middle of the road. He slammed on the brakes and his car stalled. When the terrified driver frantically tried to get the car going, it refused to start. The figure walked behind the car just as Pettijohn was able to turn over his car engine and speed away.

Although this case is suggestive, it is also possible that Pettijohn had stalled his car by braking too hard and then flooded the engine in his haste to get the car running again.

Another fact which indicates that these various creatures are psychic beings is their relationship to UFOs. Several UFO experts have noted that strange creatures are often reported during UFO waves. Of course, there are several possible explanations for this relationship. The creatures might come from the UFOs, or perhaps whatever causes the UFOs also causes the monsters (indicating psychic projections). On the other hand, people are more likely to *report* monster sightings during UFO waves, and these reports are more likely to get into print. It is also possible that during UFO epidemics people become suggestible and start "seeing things." One can take his pick among these theories.

Like UFOs, however, odd creatures seem to come in waves. Whole towns or farmlands will suddenly become replete with monster sightings as newspapers or law enforcement agencies, one after another, are flooded with reports. One typical epidemic peaked during 1966–7 in the Ohio Valley when all sorts of people began seeing Mothman, a huge bat-winged man-creature. John Keel investigated the sightings and reported them in his *Strange Creatures from*

Time and Space and later in his book *The Mothman Prophecies.*

Whatever Mothman was, or is, I don't think it was physical. Even before the Ohio Valley epidemic, there had been sightings of Mothman. In 1956, Gray Barker, a noted UFO buff, reported a 1953 case from Houston, Texas. This Mothman appears to have been apparitional. A Mrs. Walker and two anonymous witnesses watched a torpedo-shaped object swoosh down and land on her pecan tree. She described it as a glowing "figure of a man with wings like a bat. He was dressed in gray or black tight-fitting clothes." The glow began to fade and the creature disappeared.

During the 1966-7 wave, several people saw a similar monster. On September 1, several people saw a manlike object flying in the sky at a low altitude. One month later, a National Guardsman saw a brown manlike creature in a tree. That same month, two married couples saw a "large gray man-shape creature with blazing red eyes, 10-foot wing span." The monster chased the viewers' automobile. A few days later, two firemen saw the same being in the same area. Housewives, teen-agers, and even pilots eventually confronted the bat-winged man-monster. By November, 1967, the sightings began to fade out. Most reports came from Point Pleasant, West Virginia.

Was this a real creature or not? Some indications about the nature of the Mothman can be gleaned by taking a closer look at those who saw it. One of the first witnesses was Mrs. Mabel McDaniel. Her daughter had also seen the creature. What happened afterward was a virtual nightmare, according to Keel:

> The McDaniel family had been living in the twilight zone ever since their daughter and the others had first glimpsed "Mothman." Linda had repeatedly heard the sound of a speeded-up phonograph record around her own home after the incident, and peculiar manifestations indicating the presence of a poltergeist began. Finally she and Roger moved into the basement apartment in the McDaniels' home. The poltergeist followed them. Strange lights appeared in the house, objects moved by themselves, and the heavy odor of cigar smoke was frequently noted ...

These are all typical poltergeist antics. So typical, in fact, that one can't exclude the possibility that Mothman was an apparition and part of the poltergeist itself. In looking back into historical poltergeist lore, one can find many reports of grotesque animal-like apparitions that were seen in infested homes. Since in the fifteenth and sixteenth centuries poltergeists were thought to be caused by witchcraft or enchantment, no doubt the minds that projected the poltergeist also produced apparitions of witches' familiars or elementals right in keeping with the current cultural expectations. In other words, since the victims *expected* to see grotesque elementals, the PK force considerately obliged. Today, when we no longer ascribe PK outbreaks to demons or witchcraft, these grotesque apparitions are no longer reported. Could Mothman be a modern version of this phenomenon? Several other poltergeists were reported from the Ohio Valley by Mothman witnesses during 1966–7 as well.

While Keel feels that Mothman was some form of independent entity, he made two observations on the basis of his investigations which support my psychic theory. First, Keel notes: "About half the witnesses appeared to be people with latent or active psychic abilities, prone to having accurate premonitions, prophetic dreams, extrasensory perceptions (ESP), etc."

UFO activity was also on the increase in the Ohio Valley during the Mothman invasion and Keel writes, "As the UFO activity seemed to increase, the 'Mothman' reports dwindled off."

These two statements are extremely revealing. First, it seems that those who most readily saw Mothman were psychic to begin with and so had the requisite "energy" (whatever that means) to create the being. Secondly, since there seems to have been a relationship between Mothman and UFO activity (mostly glowing lights seen in the sky), could Mothman and the UFOs have been psychic projections, one of which transformed into the other?

As a matter of fact, I came very close to seeing one of these UFOs myself. I was living in the Ohio Valley during these incidents, about 150 miles from Point Pleasant. I was too busy with college studies and "respectable" parapsychology to have been interested in the Mothman reports, but one night in February (shortly after the Mothman furor ended and the UFO activity was in its glory) a UFO appeared right over the college dorm where I was living. Witnesses testified that the glowing orb almost instantaneously zipped over the campus to its far north side (a distance of about a quarter of a mile) and zoomed off. I didn't see the light myself, as I was writing in the dorm at the time, but several students excitedly told me about the incident the next morning.

The primary finding about Mothman was that most sightings of him seemed to occur around an old TNT dump at Point Pleasant. Here large munition domes spread over the countryside for several square miles. If Mothman had a home, so to speak, this area must have been its nesting place. This may give us a clue to the nature of Mothman.

With all these bits and pieces of data, I think we can offer a unified explanation for the Mothman invasion. Something inhabited the TNT area. Whether it was a mass of psychic energy, a normal animal, or even an imaginary creature is something I don't know. But gradually, as more and more people encountered or thought they encountered "it," they projected a thought-image which eventually became molded into Mothman. Thus, Mothman was a psychic creature constantly fed by the thoughts, PK, and near-hysteria of the Ohio Valley residents. Usually poltergeists inhabit or plague a home. Yet other poltergeists will travel to neighbors, follow those who confront it, and sometimes, as in one German case I know of, an entire city block will be invaded. Mothman too began to spread out from the munitions dump. The first sightings could have been imaginary or psychic projections. But as hysteria gripped Point Pleasant, and later the entire Ohio Valley, Mothman spread as psychic thought-forms were released or fed by the hysterical. In other words, the residents *created* the exact thing they feared or heard about. Mothman was a psychically projected nighmare. The PK energy that gave rise to the creature may also have given rise to the glowing orbs of lights seen in the same area. Finally, as the frenzy receded, Mothman disappeared, leaving behind only the free-floating aerial lights.

Actually Mothman is like a hellish version of Zeitoun. I suggested that at Zeitoun the worshippers themselves created a psychic blueprint of the Virgin which finally objectified into an intelligent but often robotlike phantom. Mothman could have been the same thing—the objectification of all the gargoylish archetype monsters housed in our own unconscious. But this time one of these mental gargoyles escaped from the realm of fantasy into objective existence.

Many astonished psychics have recorded this "objectification of thought" occurring on a small scale. The most famous and often quoted case comes from the Tibetan traveler Mme. Alexandra David-Neel, who in her memoirs, *Magic and Mys-*

tery in Tibet, tells how she decided to create an apparitional thought-form of a jovial monk. This thought-form, unfortunately, broke away from her control and took on a threatening, nefarious disposition, and was even *seen by other people* before it was finally destroyed. I feel that Mothman could have been a creation drawn from and produced by many minds.

Actually, we may not have seen the last of Mothman. Even as I write, there is a flurry of reports from Texas of a huge flying creature with a ten-foot wingspan and a bat-like or monkey-like face. The creature has now been seen by several independent witnesses.

Mothman is only one creature that may have escaped from fantasy or nightmare into reality. If a place is associated by legend or tradition with a supernatural creature, could not the legend eventually emerge as fact? If a forest area allegedly houses a Bigfoot within its flora and fauna, could not the hundreds of people who come yearly to hunt it actually built up a psychically projected apparition of the beast? This would explain why abominable snowmen and their ilk are seen in certain areas, yet never leave droppings, regurgitated food, or their buried dead.

John C. Lawson, a noted forklorist and traveler, hit upon a similar principle. In talking about naiads, dryads, and other nymphs in his *Modern Greek Folklore and Ancient Greek Religion*, Lawson said he would not dismiss the possibility that there was a reality behind these legends:

> . . . Nor is it [the belief in nymphs] a matter of faith only; more than once I have been in villages where certain nereids were known by sight to several persons (so at least they averred); and there was a wonderful agreement among the witnesses in the description of their appearance and dress. I myself once had a Nereid pointed out to me by my guide, and there certainly was the semblance of a female figure draped in white and tall beyond human stature flitting in the dusk between the gnarled and twisted boles of an old olive yard. What the apparition was, I had no leisure to investigate, for my guide with many signs of the cross and muttered invocations of the Virgin ordered my mule to perilous haste along the rough mountain path.

What did Lawson see? Was it a true nymph or was it a psychic blueprint that had been animated through the thoughts and beliefs of the Greek locals?

Monsters, Bigfoot, Mothman—these creatures may all have psychic explanations. But our world is also haunted by further mysteries—mysteries that have no psychic explanation and which lead to a ghastly possibility: are there intelligences on earth, other than our own, affecting humankind?

Many UFO and Fortean buffs believe that all the manifestations I have been talking about are caused by an alien intelligence—not necessarily extraterrestrial, just alien. This is, admittedly, an entirely different but valid way of looking at the Fortean problem. Is some bizarre intelligence behind the UFOs manifesting before us as at Zeitoun and Fatima, teleporting people away, throwing objects on the earth, and creating monsters for us to see?

There can be little doubt that some Fortean events do show intelligence. Take UFOs, for example. Jacques Vallee, John Keel, and others have pointed out the absurdity of many UFO sightings. The following report is fictitious but almost identical to many that have been given: John Doe and his wife are driving along a country road when they see two silvery midgets collecting rocks and repairing their UFO right smack in the middle of the highway. The occupants see the travelers, wave at them, and scurry off. The entire incident is shrouded by mysteries. The UFO was in the middle of the highway, even though UFOs give a superficial appearance of wishing to hide. It was as though it really *wanted* to be seen. In other words, what John Doe saw was a drama intelligently staged for his benefit! This "show and tell" element in UFO reports is quite common. Jacques Vallee has collected many reports of interactions between humans and aliens. Usually the aliens ask completely ridiculous questions such as "What time is it?" Again, an element of absurdity is introduced.

From 1966–8, the Uintah Basin in Utah was the scene of a gigantic UFO flap. Discs, lights, Saturn-shaped objects all seemed to be patrolling the area. State University of Utah biologist Frank Salisbury analyzed all the sightings and had to conclude, "I can't believe that the Uintah Basin witnesses were just accidental observers of the activities of extraterrestrial beings who were systematically engaged in the business of exploring our planet. Rather, the UFOs seemed to be putting on a show, a display *aimed specifically at the witnesses.*" This implies intelligence.

Miracles too show an intelligence of their own. At Zeitoun and Fatima, the apparitions appeared to be living, self-cogni-

A Psychic Look at Foreteana 157

zant creations. At Fatima the apparition instructed the children, and at Zeitoun it acknowledged the greeting of the crowds.

Jacques Vallee believes that miracles, UFOs, and religious revelations are all aspects of a "control system"—some form of intelligence manifesting in different ways according to the current cultural expectation which manipulates man's global consciousness. John Keel's contribution to this general idea is a little more frightening. He believes that we are being controlled and manipulated by an intelligence which seeks to trick, annoy, and harass man by confronting him with all sorts of bizarre and self-contradictory information. He calls the intelligences "the mimics of man." The way UFOs have historically echoed normal technology would be a typical example of what Keel believes to be this intelligence's manner of harrassment.

All through the literature of Forteana one senses an intelligence at work, an intelligence that is no mere psychic projection. Ivan Sanderson called them "the Invisibles," and felt that man could be influenced by invisible beings that share the earth with him. Popular writer Brad Steiger calls them "the tricksters" ... beings which perpetually seek to trick and befuddle man. Even Charles Fort once exclaimed, "We are property!"

One of the most widely recognized manifestations of this intelligence is the men-in-black syndrome. Many UFO witnesses and investigators have encountered the MIBs. Witnesses might find them on their doorsteps, or investigators might find them at their offices. In each case, from one to three men dressed in black appear, usually driving a black Cadillac, and threaten or harass the investigators or witnesses. Sometimes they have detailed knowledge about their victim's activities. A UFO witness, for example, who had revealed *nothing about his sighting to anyone*, might be confronted by these men who would show that they were fully acquainted with even the most intricate aspects of the sighting and the witness's subsequent actions! MIB cases have been reported from all over the world. In 1956, Gray Barker even wrote a bizarre book, *They Knew Too Much About Flying Saucers*, when he discovered that UFO investigators around the world had been visited by the MIBs.

As in the case of mysterious disappearances, it is hard to put much stock in these MIB cases unless one has some personal involvement with them or with someone who has. I've never met an MIB, but I was able to hear about and investigate one case that was reported to me in 1975. Hitherto, it had been easy to dismiss MIB reports as lies, paranoid delusions, or the product of some out-for-some-fun pranksters. The reporter of this case must remain anonymous, as he is a well-known scientist (whose name would be familar to most people reading this book) who during his high school and college days was an amateur UFO investigator and even organized an investigating society. I'll call him Dr. R.

Dr. R. and his associates had been intensively investigating UFO sightings in one of the southern states, and their results and reports were usually presented at local meetings of the society. However, the day before one such meeting, Dr. R.'s co-investigator, a psychic in his own right, warned that the meeting was going to be disrupted by a nefarious and mysterious man and that he (Dr. R.) must do all in his power to keep himself composed. Oddly, *another* associate reported to Dr. R. a similar psychic impression he had received about a disrupting influence due at the next meeting. The stage had been set.

The next day, the meeting was held as scheduled. However, before it got underway, Dr. R. noticed a strange, tall, evil-looking man loitering near the meeting room. The man acted very peculiarly, and since he was dressed in a long black overcoat, Dr. R. and his associates laughed about his resemblance to the typical MIB. He had never been seen at the meetings before.

As the meeting began and the latest reports and news were presented, the prediction came true. The MIB stood up and directly challenged Dr. R. about his work, activity, and plans. He had intimate knowledge of private UFO reports filed with Dr. R. and was even familiar with an out-of-the-country trip that Dr. R. was planning to take—a secret that had been closely guarded. Dr. R. was amazed at his knowledge and to this day has no explanation as to how the man got his information. Dr. R. stood his ground, and the foreigner sat down, but the intimidation was not over.

After the meeting, as Dr. R. and his friends started to drive to a friend's house, the MIB followed them. A wild chase ensued, and Dr. R. believes the man would have tried to run them off the road had they not outmaneuvered him. He vanished after that and never appeared again.

This report is typical of the MIB syndrome. Similar cases have been reported for years. In short, MIBs are presences who appear out of nowhere, have paranormal knowledge of their victims' lives, and vanish just as mysteriously. Some intelligence is at work!

On this problem, Dr. Berthold Schwarz has written:

> The whole question of MIBs ... is most difficult to analyze ... The borderline between psychopathology, coincidence, telepathy, and synchronicity, and possible MIB events is very poorly defined. The author was very surprised to learn from interviews with several respected Ufologists that MIB phenomena happen rarely, or never at all. However, on further pointed questioning, it was learned that one of these people indeed had some excellent examples of MIBs but had consciously dismissed the material because it would contaminate his studies, was too weird to be considered, or was irrelevant to the problem of UFOs ... one must ... have a technique of getting at the information before we conclude that it doesn't exist. This latter policy can only be an example of the investigator's inexperience or ignorance of the phenomena at hand, rather than its nonexistence.

Another form of intelligent harassment is by way of the phone. UFO witnesses are often subject to weird phone calls, even if they have unlisted numbers. They are threatened, or the callers claim to be people known to them, but then slip up, revealing that they are only mimics. Weird bleeping sounds come over the lines as well. Berthold Schwarz has investigated two cases of this phenomenon. In both of them, the UFO witnesses received mysterious calls warning them not to discuss their encounters. In one case, the family of witnesses received the call at their unlisted number before they had even told outsiders about their previous UFO encounter!

This telephonic high-jinx is so common that it represents a pattern in its own right. As Keel points out, the intelligence behind the phone call will often mimic real persons. Some of the cases do sound like practical jokes, but others are more complex. Here is a typical case of phone harrassment reported by John Keel in *The Mothman Prophecies*:

> I spent most of March, 1968, in Washington, D.C. While I was gone, an old Army buddy, a serious, quiet man who worked in advertising, stayed in my apartment. He was totally reliable and not a practical joker. When I returned, I found a stack of messages from phone calls he had received while I was gone. One was from George Clark, a UFO en-

thusiast in New Jersey. He had called on March 23 and asked for me to call him back. I never got around to it. So a few days later he called again and I apologized for not returning his previous call. There was a stunned silence on the other end and then he slowly told me that I *had* called him back around 10 P.M. on March 27. A voice that sounded exactly like mine had talked to him at length, using my pet expressions and noncommittal statements such as, "Well, we'll just have to wait and see what happens next."

Two days later, George said he called my number again around 8 P.M. and a "hippie" answered. "No, man, Mr. Keel ain't here right now ... but he ought to back soon. Would you like to leave a message, man?" George left a message with him.

That particular evening I was back in New York and sitting next to my phone.

What is going on here? Telephone malfunction or a practical joke ... or something more?

Once again I have to repeat: these cases seem easy to dismiss until one has some firsthand experience with them. On three occasions I've run into odd telephone incidents in my own home. I can neither dismiss nor explain them. They are totally baffling and in fact I rarely mention them because they are so bizarre. But now I would like to place them on record.

The first case alerted me to the phenomenon in 1974. I had just moved into a new home in a pleasant Los Angeles suburb. I had spent the summer before doing research at a parapsychology laboratory back East where I had worked with Dr. Robert Morris, a well-known experimental parapsychologist. I had learned that Bob was going to be in San Francisco, and I thought I might drive up to see him. I had a friend a few blocks away who I thought would want to make the trip with me, so I drove over to discuss the matter with him and then tried to get in touch with Bob. Both ventures were unsuccessful. Then I drove back home. I was gone no more than an hour.

Later that day, a friend of mine named Tony called. He was trying to get in touch with his brother Gary, a college student who was renting a room from me at the back of the house. He was angry. "Didn't you give Gary my message?" he said sternly. I didn't know what he was talking about. Then the story emerged. Tony had placed a call to my house when I was away through an operator since he could not dial out directly on the phone he was using. A man had answered.

He denied being Gary or me (we both have similar voices over the phone) but offered the information that his name was "Bob," and that he was a friend of mine. He took the message Tony gave and that ended the conversation. Odd indeed! I am gone for only an hour trying to reach Bob in San Francisco, and a mysterious "Bob" answers my phone at home and seems rather conversant with me and my tenant! Was this all a bizarre coincidence? A wrong number to a house where a "Scott" and a "Gary" just happened to live? It is possible.

But a few months later the same thing happened! Bob was coming to L.A. and I had to leave to make arrangements for his arrival. I was gone a total of twenty minutes. It was the only time I was out of the house during the entire day. That evening my colleague Raymond Bayless called. Angrily he asked, "Didn't Gary give you my message to call me back?" This startled me since my tenant had been gone all day and had just gotten back. Here is the story as we pieced it out. By comparing times, we were able to determine that Raymond had called during the twenty minutes that I was gone. A young man answered and acknowledged Raymond's voice and obviously knew who he was. He told Raymond that I was out, and they spoke briefly. Raymond was sure that the voice was identical to Gary's. But nobody was home! Once again, this incident occurred when I was out on errands concerning Bob Morris, so the coincidence is staggering. In both cases, the answerers were completely aware of who I was, who Gary was, and held consistent conversations with the callers. Apparently the voice was even like ours. I had Raymond speak to Gary over the phone immediately after I heard the story. Again, Raymond adamantly declared that the voices were identical. An independent witness did prove that Gary was in San Bernardino County that day—all day.

The last incident occurred only two months ago as I write. I had phoned the UCLA Neuropsychiatric Institute to talk with Dr. Thelma Moss but had been unable to reach her and instead spoke with one of her assistants, Bary Taff. At 4:00 that day I was lying on my living room couch thinking about calling her back but was too lazy to get up to do so. At 6:00 that evening, Barry called me back, explaining that he was "answering my message." "What message," I asked. It seems that at 4:00 someone called Dr. Moss' lab and left my name, saying to call back.

Usually one can find a psychic explanation for just about

any mystery. But these phone manipulations are so bizarre that I have no possible explanation for them. Yet again, this mimicry follows a pattern. Compare these cases with a series of similar incidents reported by Keel:

> At 1 A.M. on the morning of Friday, July 14, 1967, I received a call from a man who identified himself as Gray Barker from West Virginia. The voice sounded exactly like Gray's softly accented mellifluous own, but he addressed me as if I were a total stranger and carefully called me "Mr. Keel." At first I wondered if maybe he hadn't been out celebrating. The quiet, familiar drawl told me that he knew I wrote for newspapers and he had just heard about a case which he thought I should look into. It was, he said, similar to the Deren*stein* case. Gray and I had visited Woodrow Derenberger together, so I knew this was not the kind of mistake he would make.
>
> Around that time I had received a number of reports from people in the New York area who had been receiving nuisance calls from a woman who identified herself as "Mrs. Gray Barker." I knew that Gray was not married, but when I mentioned these calls to this "Gray Barker," he paused for a moment and then said, "No, Mrs. Barker hasn't been calling anybody up there." He returned to his recital of an absurdly insignificant UFO sighting near West Mifflin, Pennsylvania. It was not the kind of incident that would have inspired a long-distance call. Later I did try to check it out and found all the information he gave me was false.
>
> We talked for about ten minutes and throughout that period "Gray" sounded like a man under duress . . . as though someone was holding a gun to his head. I tricked him several times with different meaningless references and by the time I hung up I was definitely convinced that this man was not the real Gray Barker.
>
> An hour later, my phone rang again and a young man said, "Gray *Baker* has been trying to reach you . . . he asked us to give you this number and to please call him." He recited a number that was identical to my own except for the last digit.
>
> There were more calls from strangers that night, and more pointless messages from Gray *Baker*.
>
> The next day, I called Gray long distance and he denied having placed the call, naturally.
>
> Soon after that, I discovered that another "John Keel" had been phoning people around the country, imitating my voice and mannerisms exactly. Mary Hyre received one such call. I phoned her a few days afterward and she said, "I'm glad

you're feeling better ... you sounded sick or drunk the other night."

"What other night?"

"When you called a couple of nights ago. Remember we talked about your letter and what you thought was going to happen on the river."*

I had not called her and discussed the letter. Nor had I discussed the disaster prediction with anyone other than the contactees who were told about it.

If these calls were a joke, they were purposeless. Yet, the level of mimicry is astounding. The knowledge the calls revealed seems paranormal, and this proves that no totally normal explanation could account for them. Consider how that call to UCLA echoed my private thoughts! Did I confront "the trickster," or "the mimics of man?"

I am afraid that this book must end on a note of mystery. Just as there are all sorts of uncanny things haunting our planet, there are perhaps alien intelligences invading it as well. Maybe they are mimics—mimics representing a mirror-image of our own minds. Or perhaps MIBs and phantom phone-callers represent a phenomenon so bizarre and complicated that our mortal minds could never hope to understand it.

At the beginning of this book, I said that one should not promote a theory unless one could test it experimentally, either to verify it or to negate it. Perhaps I have violated that principle several times in the course of these chapters. If so, it is only because when confronting something so extraordinary as a miracle we can never explore it experimentally. All we can do is make deductions from our observations. As the Oxford philosopher H. H. Price once said about our probings into the unknown: "... we may safely predict that it will be the timidity of our hypotheses and not their extravagance which will provoke the derision of posterity."

I do not know what further research will prove about all the theories and speculations I have outlined in this book. They might all prove to be false. On the other hand, I shall be delighted if eventually science discovers that I am right!

---

* This refers to predictions of the collapse of the Silver Bridge over the Ohio River which cost several motorists their lives in the late 1960s.

Bibliography

Chapter 2 The Mystery of Teleportation

Bayless, Raymond, *Experiences of a Psychical Researcher*. New Hyde Park: University Books, 1972.
Blatty, Peter, *I'll Tell Them I Remember You*. New York: W. W. Norton, 1973.
Carrington, Hereward, "Mysterious Disappearances," *Psychic Research*, December, 1930.
Fodor, Nandor, *Mind Over Space*. New York: Citadel Press, 1962.
Fort, Charles, *The Books of Charles Fort*. New York: Henry Holt, 1941.
Gaddis, Vincent, *Invisible Horizons*. Radnor, Pa.: Chilton, 1965.
Hack, Gwendolyn Kelly, *Modern Psychic Mysteries*. London: Rider, n.d.
Keel, John, *Our Haunted Planet*. Greenwich, Conn.: Fawcett, 1971.
Lapponi, Joseph, *Ipnotismo e Spiritismo*. Rome: 1906.
van Loon, L. H., "Some Unusual Psychokinetic Phenomena Associated with the Recovery of Lost Objects," in J. C. Poynton's (ed.) *Parapsychology in South Africa*, Johannesburg: South African Society for Psychical Research, 1975.
Maliwang, Vincent, "Manila's Disappearing Boy," *Fate*, August, 1965.
Mowbray, C. W., *Transition*, second edition. London: L.S.A. Publications Ltd., 1947.
Paulmer, Stuart, "How Lost Was My Father," *Fate*, July, 1953.
Sanderson, Ivan T., *Uninvited Visitors*. New York: Cowles, 1967.
Sanderson, Ivan T., "The Spreading Mystery of the Bermuda Triangle," *Argosy*, August, 1968.
Sanderson, Ivan T., *Invisible Residents*. New York: World Publishing Co., 1970.
Steiger, Brad, "People Are Disappearing," *Probe the Unknown*, May, 1975.

Chapter 3 Mysteries and Miracles

Bayless, Raymond, "Investigating a Weeping Icon," *Fate*, March, 1966.

Clark, Jerome, and Coleman, Loren, *The Unidentified*. New York: Warner Paperback Library, 1975.

Feilding, Everard, "The Case of Abbé Vachère," in *Sittings with Eusapia Palladino and Other Studies*. New Hyde Park: University Books, 1963.

Fodor, Nandor, *Between Two Worlds*. West Nyack, N.Y.: Parker, 1964.

Fort, Charles, *Wild Talents*. New York: Ace, n.d.

Fryer, A. T., "Psychological Aspects of the Welsh Revival," *Proceedings of the Society for Psychical Research* 1905-7, 19, 80-167.

Gillese, John, "The Virgin's Visit to Garabandal, Part 1, *Fate*, December, 1965; Part 2, *Fate*, January, 1966.

Giorgi, Giorgio, *"Fede, Scienza, Parasicologia di Fronte al Miracolo di Gennaro"* (Faith, Science, and Parapsychology Confronting the Miracle of St. Januarius), *Quaderni di Parapsicologia*, 1970, 1, 18-28.

Lambert, Helen, *A General Survey of Psychical Phenomena*. New York: Knickerbocker Press, 1928.

Lloyd, Jerome, "In a Little Spanish Town," *Probe*, Winter, 1974.

Lozano, Rafael, "The Troubles a 'Miracle' Brought," *Life*, July 26, 1962.

Palmer, Jerome, *Our Lady Returns to Egypt*. San Bernardino, Calif.: Culligan Publications, 1969.

Palmer, Jerome, "The Virgin Mary Appears in Egypt," *Fate*, August, 1971.

Rauscher, William, with Spraggett, Allen, *The Spiritual Frontier*. Garden City, N.Y.: Doubleday, 1975.

Rogo, D. Scott, *An Experience of Phantoms*. New York: Taplinger, 1974.

Roll, W. G. *The Poltergeist*. New York: New American Library, 1974.

Techter, David, "A Flap of Glowing Crosses," *Fate*, June, 1972.

Thomas, Paul, *Flying Saucers Through the Ages*. London: Neville Spearman, 1962.

Tweedale, Charles, *News from the Next World*. London: Psychic Book Club, n.d.

Walsh, William, *Our Lady of Fatima*. Garden City: Image Books, 1954 (original publication, 1947).

Chapter 4   UFOs: Space Vehicles or Psychic Entities?

Bayless, Raymond, *Experiences of a Psychical Investigator*. New Hyde Park: University Books, 1972.

Bernard, Raymond, *The Hollow Earth*. New York: Dell, 1975.

Bond, Bryce, "An Interview with Ivan Sanderson," *Psychic Observer*. March, 1974.

Clark, Jerome, and Coleman, Loren, *The Unidentified*. New York: Warner Paperback Library, 1975.

Creighton, Gordon, "Healing from UFOs," *Flying Saucer Review*. September-October, 1969.

Druffel, Anne, "The Yorba Linda Photograph," *Flying Saucer Review*, November, 1973.

Eisenbud, Jule, *The World of Ted Serios*. New York: Morrow, 1966.

Gratton-Guinness, I., "A Note on the Significance of Stella Lansing," *Flying Saucer Review*. Vol. 21, No. 2, 1975.

Hynek, J. Allen, *The UFO Experience: A Scientific Inquiry*. Chicago: Regnery Co., 1972.

James, Trevor, *They Live in the Sky*. Los Angeles: New Age Publishing Co., 1958.

James, Trevor (Trevor James Constable), "The Case for the "Critters'," in Steiger, B., and White, J. (eds.) *Other Worlds, Other Universes*. Garden City, N.Y.: Doubleday, 1975.

Jung, C. J., *Flying Saucers: A Modern Myth of Things Seen in the Sky*. New York: Harcourt, Brace & World, 1959.

Keel, John, "Mystery Airplanes of the 1930s," *Flying Saucer Review*, May-June, 1970, July-August, 1970.

Michel, Aimé, "The Strange Case of Dr. 'X,'" *Flying Saucer Review*, September 1969—Special issue No. 3.

Michel, Aimé, *The Truth about Flying Saucers*. New York: Pyramid Books, 1974.

Sanderson, Ivan, *Invisible Residents*. New York: World, 1970.

Sanderson, Ivan, *Uninvited Visitors*. New York: Cowles, 1967.

Schönherr, Luis, "The Question of Reality," *Flying Saucer Review*, March-April, 1971.

Schwarz, Berthold, "The Port Monmouth Landing," *Flying Saucer Review*, May-June, 1971.

Schwarz, Berthold, "Stella Lansing's UFO Motion Picture," *Flying Saucer Review*, January-February, 1972.

Schwarz, Berthold, "Stella Lansing's Clocklike UFO Patterns," *Flying Saucer Review*, Vol. 20, Nos. 4,5,6; Vol. 21, No. 1.

Schwarz, Berthold, "Woodstock UFO Festival," *Flying Saucer Review*, January-February, 1973; March-April, 1973.

Trench, Brinsley Le Poer, *Mysterious Visitors*. New York: Stein & Day, n.d.

Vallee, Jacques, *The Invisible College*. New York: Dutton, 1975.

Chapter 5 Pascagoula Revisited: The Psychic Story

Blum, Ralph and Judy, *Beyond Earth: Man's Contact with UFOs*. New York: Bantam Books, 1974.

Clark, Jerome, and Coleman, Loren, *The Unidentified*. New York: Warner Paperback Library, 1975.

Fuller, John, *The Interrupted Journey.* New York: Dial, 1966.
P.S.I. "The Charles Hickson—P.S.I. Sighting," *P.S.I.: Journal of Instrumental UFO Research,* Vol. 1, 1975, 13-15.
Vallee, Jacques, *The Invisible College.* New York: Dutton, 1975.
——— "Arizona Man Captured by UFO," *National Enquirer,* December 16, 1975.

Chapter 6 The Cosmic Invaders

Bartell, Jan Bryant, *Spindrift.* New York: New American Library, 1975.
Bayless, Raymond, *Experiences of a Psychical Researcher.* New Hyde Park, N.Y.: University Books, 1972.
Guirdham, Arthur, *Obsession.* London: Neville Spearman, 1972.
Keel, John, *The Mothman Prophecies.* New York: Saturday Review Press, 1975.
Le Leau, Esther, "An Unusual and Recurrent Experience," *Journal of the American Society for Psychical Research,* 1951, 45, 158-65.
Lethbridge, Tom, *Ghost and Divining Rod.* London: Routledge & Kegan Paul.
London, Perry, and Rosenham, David (eds.), *Foundations of Abnormal Psychology.* New York: Holt, Rinehart & Winston, 1968.

Chapter 7 A Psychic Look at Forteana

Barker, Gray, *They Knew Too Much About Flying Saucers.* New York: University Books, 1956.
Clark, Jerome, and Coleman, Loren, *The Unidentified.* New York: Warner Paperback Library, 1975.
Keel, John, *Our Haunted Planet.* Greenwich, Conn.: Fawcett, 1971.
Keel, John, *Strange Creatures from Time and Space.* Greenwich, Conn.: Fawcett, 1970.
Keel, John, *The Mothman Prophecies.* New York: Saturday Review Press/Dutton, 1975.
Salisbury, Frank, *The Utah UFO Display.* Old Greenwich, Conn.: Devin-Adair, 1974.
Schwarz, Berthold, "Stella Lansing's UFO Motion Pictures," *Flying Saucer Review,* Vol. 18, No. 1, 1972.

Printed in the United States
216482BV00001B/9/A